FREE TO THRIVE

40 POWER-PACKED DEVOTIONS FOR WOMEN ON THE GO

ANDREA LENNON

True Vine Ministry
Conway, Arkansas

I dedicate this book to you, the reader.

I love you, and I thank God for the fact that He allows me
to invest in your life through His Word. I want you to know that
I really believe that you can be *free to thrive*! God loves you, and
He has a plan for your life. Each day embrace Him and know that
you will experience the freedom that comes from
knowing, loving, and serving Jesus Christ!

I invite you to connect with me
via my website: www.andrealennon.net

About the Author

Andrea Lennon

Andrea Lennon was born in Searcy, Arkansas, in March 1976. She spent her first few days of life in a hospital waiting for her parents, James and Sandra Morris, to pick her up for adoption.

From a very early age, Andrea loved going to church and felt at home with the people of God. As a six-year-old, Andrea received Jesus Christ as her personal Lord and Savior during a revival at First Baptist Church in Paris, Arkansas. God called Andrea to serve Him in ministry when she was eighteen, but Andrea did not respond to His call at that time.

In 1996, Andrea married Jay Lennon; after a year of marriage, they settled in Conway, Arkansas. They established a routine of going to church on Sunday and living like the world the rest of the week. This went on for some time but soon became unfulfilling. Both Jay and Andrea knew something was missing in their lives. It did not take them long to figure out that it was not something but Someone—the Lord Jesus. Jay and Andrea began seeking the Lord, and soon their lives changed radically. During this time, God called Andrea a second time to serve Him in ministry, and praise His name, she responded yes!

Andrea always knew she was called to teach women the Word of God. In the fall of 2005, Andrea began leading women's ministry events. Since that time, her passion for teaching God's Word has grown. Andrea's desire is to honor the Lord by living out His Word in her own life and then challenging other women to do so as well.

In 2007 Andrea established True Vine Ministry for the purpose of reaching and discipling women in Jesus Christ. The Lord has faithfully opened doors at home and abroad for her to do this. Today Andrea praises God for the opportunities to invest in the lives of women. Andrea's heart is to encourage women to know the truth, live the truth, and share the truth.

Jay and Andrea Lennon live in Conway, Arkansas, with their sons, Jake and Andrew.

Contents

FREE TO THRIVE

40 Power-packed Devotions for Women on the Go

Welcome to *Free to Thrive!* This devotion book was created just for you. If you are like me, you know what it is like to live a busy life that often leaves you asking the question, "Lord, how can I make all the 'to do's' in my life fit?" It is my prayer that this devotion book will help you answer that question. I invite you to use *Free to Thrive* to have a meaningful quiet time even on days when you feel pressed for time.

The formula for each devotion time is simple. Each day you will be asked to Read It, Think About It, and Respond To It. This simple approach allows you to look closely at a spiritual truth and then respond to that truth in your daily life. The 40 devotions are power packed and designed to speak to the hearts of those who long to have freedom in their lives. Galatians 5:1 is the key verse for this study. "It is for freedom that Christ has set us free. Stand firm, then, and do not let yourselves be burdened again by a yoke of slavery."

Galatians 5:1 teaches that freedom is available today! In fact, Jesus valued your freedom so much that He gave His life in order to secure it. This truth should cause you to stop and think about the amount of freedom you experience. No longer do you have to remain bound up in slavery by giving in to the influences of this world. Jesus Christ has purchased your freedom and offers it to you!

It is time to begin this adventure. Please know that I love you, and I am fighting for you. I value your freedom in Christ, and I want you to know that I am on your side. The next eight weeks might change your life deeply. I find that very exciting, and I know you do too! Please allow me the honor of praying for you as you begin this adventure.

Dear Lord,

I praise Your holy name! Lord, You alone are worthy of praise. I want to come to You now to pray for my dear sister. As she begins this spiritual adventure, help her to remain diligent to spend time with You in Your Word even during the busy days of life. Give her a steadfast heart. Thank You that You created my sister to be free. What an amazing thought! I pray that over the next eight weeks, my sister will be changed as she embraces Your freedom for life. Lord, help her to thrive no matter what life brings her way. In Jesus' name I pray, amen.

Much love!

Andrea Lennon

Week 1:
A Biblical Introduction to Freedom

"We are free to thrive when we embrace God's definition of freedom."

Day 1:
A New Definition of Freedom

"It is for freedom that Christ has set us free. Stand firm, then, and do not let yourselves be burdened again by a yoke of slavery."

Galatians 5:1

Read It

Today's culture needs a new definition of freedom—a definition based on biblical truth. Believers in Jesus Christ grossly misunderstand freedom when they buy into the world's definition of freedom by thinking that freedom means independence from any limitations of time, money, relationships, and consequences. This misunderstanding occurs when a believer thinks that they are free when they are able to do what they want to do, when they want to do it, and have the resources available to make things happen. According to the Bible, freedom has nothing to do with earthly things. The Bible teaches that freedom is found in Jesus Christ. In fact, for the believer, freedom is living a life of total abandon to Jesus Christ. We are free to thrive when we are liberated from the effect of sin and self so we can live the life of abundance God created us to live.

Without a doubt, there is a difference between the world's definition of freedom and the Bible's definition of freedom. The world defines freedom as independence from any limitations in our daily life. The Bible defines freedom as complete dependence on Jesus Christ. Only as we depend on Him are we truly free to thrive!

In Galatians 5:1, the apostle Paul spoke directly to the freedom issue. Paul stated, "It is for freedom that Christ has set us free." Do you hear the certainty in this passage? I do. The daily question for the believer is not, "Is freedom available for me?" The true choice is, "Will I walk in the freedom Christ provides?"

Walking in the freedom Christ provides occurs as we walk with Christ. This means embracing the truth that we are on a journey that has a very definite destination. The destination is not found in this world. Rather, the destination is found in our real home with Christ in heaven. As we walk with Christ towards our heavenly destination, we experience a willingness to surrender to the things of Christ—and we are set free to thrive.

The second half of Galatians 5:1 teaches how we are to embrace the freedom Christ provides. Paul states, "Stand firm, then, and do not let yourselves be burdened again by a yoke of slavery." Paul makes a crucial point in this phrase. In order to be free, we must stand firm by living according to the truth in the Bible. Living according to the Bible forces us to forsake every lie rooted in our lives.

When we live our lives based on a lie, a yoke of slavery controls the direction of our lives. One definition of a yoke is a device laid on the neck of a defeated person. For just a moment, imagine yourself carrying a yoke. Try to feel the weight of the yoke as it presses your head down and your shoulders forward. Think about the fact that once a yoke of slavery controls your life, you are living a defeated life!

Today, I wonder if you are living a defeated life. I wonder if you have bought into a lie by embracing the world's definition of freedom. As a result, are you walking around in a state of defeat? If so, I have good news for you. Christ sets the believer free! Therefore, your freedom does NOT hinge on the world's definition of freedom. Your freedom is NOT dependent on comfortable situations or circumstances. It does NOT hinge on available resources like money, power, or influence. Your freedom was bought with the precious blood of Jesus Christ. The choice you now face is this: "Will you walk in the freedom Christ provides?" I hope your answer is "YES!"

Without a doubt, our culture needs to embrace a new definition for freedom—a definition based on the Bible. This definition calls for believers to surrender to Christ in every situation faced. In order to live in the freedom Christ provides, we must surrender to Christ's plans and live His way, not our own. We must have ardent loyalty to truth and look to heaven as our real home. Simply put, freedom must be found in Jesus Christ. Dear sister, forsake the things of this world. Forsake the world's definition of freedom and embrace the freedom that comes in knowing, loving, and serving Jesus Christ!

Think About It

Have you bought into the world's definition of freedom by thinking that freedom means independence from any and all limitations? If so, please list the specific ways:

_____

_____

_____

Do you see how the world's definition of freedom actually creates a yoke of slavery in your life? If so, please explain. _____

_____

_____

_____

_____

_____

What changes would be evident on a daily basis if you surrendered to God's definition of freedom that is found in Jesus Christ?_____

_____

_____

_____

Respond To It

Please journal a prayer asking the Lord to help you forsake the world's definition of freedom so you can embrace His definition of freedom. _____

_____

_____

_____

_____

_____

Day 2:
A Kingdom Focus

"But seek first his kingdom and his righteousness, and all these things will be given to you as well. Therefore, do not worry about tomorrow, for tomorrow will worry about itself. Each day has enough trouble of its own."

Matthew 6:33

Read It

Freedom requires a Kingdom of God focus. When we have a Kingdom focus, we take a step back and make the choice to see life from a big-picture perspective. This involves seeing the events of our life from the context of eternity as opposed to our days here on earth. When we live with Kingdom focus, our goals change. Our life is no longer about living happily ever after like the world's definition of freedom. Rather, our life becomes a passionate pursuit of righteous living as we live our lives for Jesus Christ, no matter what. The result of living with Kingdom focus is found in one word—freedom!

You see, when we live with Kingdom focus, we are set free from living for the trappings of this world. For many years, I lived for the world's trappings—the perfect house, the perfect car, the perfect marriage, the perfect kids, and the perfect bank account to fund all my dreams. You can imagine how exhausted I became by trying to chase the "American dream." May I share my findings with you? Pursuing the so-called "American dream" did not produce freedom. Instead, it produced bondage.

In Matthew 6:33 Jesus provided His followers with a clear instruction: "Seek first the Kingdom of God." This verse, nestled beautifully within the Sermon on the Mount, draws a line in the sand when it comes to Kingdom focus. This verse teaches that we cannot focus on two kingdoms. Either we will live our lives for God's eternal Kingdom or we will live our lives for the world's earthly kingdom. In God's eyes, we cannot live for both.

Living for God's eternal Kingdom produces freedom because it challenges us to see life from God's perspective, and we realize God promises to take care of us. Allow me to show you this truth in Scripture. A few verses prior to Matthew 6:33, Jesus shared why believers can focus completely on His Kingdom. Matthew 6:25 and 32 state, "Do not worry about your life, what you will eat or drink; or about your body, what you will wear…For the pagans run after all these things, and your heavenly Father knows that you need them." So what should the believer do instead of worry? Verse 33 provides the answer: "Seek first his kingdom and his righteousness, and all these things will be given to you as well."

When we seek God and live for His Kingdom, we receive everything He deems necessary for our time on this earth. Therefore, we do not have to worry about tomorrow or the day after that or the day after that or the day after that. Instead, each day we are free to faithfully seek the Lord. This seeking process becomes the very heart of our life as we experience Jesus' freedom by daily forsaking the natural tendency to worry about the things of this world like what we will eat, what we will drink, or what we will wear. Instead we will thrive as we seek first His Kingdom and know in our hearts that God will take care of us!

Think About It

Which kingdom do you live for? Take a look at the lists below. Please circle the statements that reflect your current focus. (You may circle statements in both lists.)

Living for this world's kingdom involves:
- being concerned with status and possessions
- desiring to live a problem-free life
- longing for security that comes from earthly resources
- focusing on gaining experiences we hope will lead to fulfillment.

Living for God's eternal Kingdom involves:
- forsaking the things of this world for the glory of Jesus Christ
- having no regard for our own names
- embracing risk in order to share the love of Jesus Christ with others
- living from a place of surrender that responds to Jesus in every area of life
- cultivating a sense of urgency to share God's Word and hope with others
- longing for our ultimate home in heaven
- daily dying to self.

Please summarize your findings from the lists above. _____
_____
_____
_____
_____
_____
_____

Is it hard for you to live for God's eternal Kingdom? If so, please explain your struggle.
_____
_____
_____
_____
_____

Do you fall into the trap of trying to live for both kingdoms? If so, please explain the bondage this trap creates. _____
_____
_____
_____

Respond To It

Do you long to live for God's eternal Kingdom? Yes or No

Please list specific ways you can live for God's eternal Kingdom this week. _____
_____
_____
_____
_____
_____

Journal a prayer asking the Lord to grant you a proper Kingdom focus in your life.
_____
_____
_____
_____
_____

Day 3:
A Passionate Trust

*"I waited patiently for the **Lord;** **he** turned to me and heard
my cry. **He** lifted me out of the slimy pit, out of the mud and
mire; **he** set my feet on a rock and gave me a firm place to stand.
He put a new song in my mouth, a hymn of praise to our God.
Many will see and fear and put their **trust** in the **Lord**."*

Psalm 40:1–3 (emphasis added)

Read It

Have you ever been so unsure of your next step that all you know to do is hang on to
Jesus and desperately hope that you make it through your day? In those times, you know
that if God does not get you through, you will not make it. Truly this type of life displays
a picture of passionate trust. And, contrary to every feeling inside your body, passionate
trust results in freedom. Believers in Jesus Christ are never freer than when Jesus is their
only hope—when Jesus is the only way out of the slimy pit. Think about it for just a
moment. Passionate trust requires us to crucify self-sufficiency and self-trust. The result?
We recognize that Jesus is our only hope.

King David knew about passionate trust. He knew about being in the depths of
desperation and God graciously saving him. David knew what it was like to have a
target on his back and experience God's deliverance time and time again. He also knew
about falling into sin and reaping God's holy consequences. Throughout David's life, his
experiences brought him to a place of complete desperation for God to work and move
in his life. Certainly this is a picture of passionate trust and humble transparency.

In today's passage, David has survived a life-altering situation. A life-altering situation is
one where life takes a dramatic turn and things are never the same. David experienced
many life-altering situations. One such situation occurred as a result of David sleeping
with Bathsheba, who became pregnant. In order to try to cover up the sin, David sent
for Bathsheba's husband, Uriah the Hittite. Uriah came home from war but did not sleep
with his wife, and David later had Uriah killed. David thought he got away with his sin,
but God did not miss this offense. God confronted David and sent holy consequences
into his life. Bathsheba gave birth to the child, but he became sick and died.

How did David make it through these crucial experiences? David cried out to God for
help. He cried out to God because he often found himself at a point where he could not
fix his problems. He could not correct his mistakes. David needed God to intervene and
save him from himself. In response to David's cry for help, God saved him and delivered
him from the slimy pit.

Psalm 40:1–3 is a hymn of praise from David's heart for the work God performed in his
life. Once God worked and moved, David not only renewed his passionate trust in God,

he also exclaimed that others would see the work of God and experience passionate trust in their lives as well.

Today you may be in the midst of your life-altering situation. This situation may or may not be in your life as a result of sin. Regardless of the cause, you have the chance to cry out to God for help. If you feel bound up by the uncertainty of life, not knowing what will happen next, you can find freedom in God's Word. Wait on the Lord. Hold onto the Lord. Know that the Lord will deliver you. Even if you are in the depths of desperation, God is with you. Even if nothing in your life makes sense and by all earthly accounts hope seems gone, hang on to Jesus!

Certainly passionate trust does not happen in our own strength or as a result of anything good inside us. We develop passionate trust when we dig deep in our faith and know that just like God delivered David from his painful situation, He will deliver us!

Think About It

Are you currently in a life-altering situation? If so, please explain. _____

_____

_____

_____

_____

_____

_____

In your life-altering situation, is passionate trust a part of your life? Are you asking Jesus to help you make it through your day? _____

_____

_____

_____

_____

Do those around you know about the struggles in your life? If so, do you think they see God at work in you? For just a moment, think about how God may be using your life to encourage another believer in their spiritual journey. Record your thoughts below.

_____

_____

_____

_____

_____

Respond To It

I want to invite you to rewrite Psalm 40:1–3 substituting your name in the place of David's personal pronouns. Once you have written your name in the blanks, please say the passage out loud. Commit this passage to memory and hang on to Jesus!

"_____ waited patiently for the Lord; he turned to _____ and heard _____ cry. He lifted _____ out of the slimy pit, out of the mud and mire; he set _____ feet on a rock and gave _____ a firm place to stand. He put a new song in _____ mouth, a hymn of praise to our God. Many will see and fear and put their trust in the Lord." Psalm 40:1–3

Please close with a word of prayer asking the Lord to grant you a passionate trust to hang on to Him for dear life. _____

_____

_____

_____

_____

_____

_____

_____

Day 4:
A Clear Goal

"For those God foreknew he also predestined to be conformed to the likeness of his Son."

Romans 8:29

Read It

When I was growing up, I had a favorite sleeping bag. This sleeping bag was special to me because on the front of the bag was printed my favorite superhero—Wonder Woman. Do you remember Wonder Woman? I remember her shiny red and blue outfit and the sparkling tiara in her long, black hair.

When I slept in my Wonder Woman sleeping bag, I pretended I was Wonder Woman. In my fantasy, there was no task too difficult for me, and no problem was beyond my ability to solve. As Wonder Woman, I could, in my own power, conquer the world!

Often the Wonder Woman mentality gets in the way of freedom. When believers set their sights on worldly goals and utilize human strength and power in order to accomplish them, they've fallen into the Wonder Woman trap. For just a moment, think about your goals in life. Often my daily goals are simple—cash the check at the bank, pick up a loaf of bread, pay the bills, or remember to wash a load of clothes. At other times, my goals are much more complex. These goals include being a good wife, raising my boys in a way that honors the Lord, and making an effort to be a productive member of my community.

Certainly these goals are good. We need daily goals that help us accomplish simple tasks as well as complex goals that force us to look at who we are and how we live our lives. However, in order to experience God's freedom, I think it is essential to add one goal to the top of our list. This goal is found in Romans 8:29 which states, "For those God foreknew he also predestined to **be conformed to the likeness of his Son**" (emphasis added). Based on this verse, we can know that God's plan for our life involves conformity to the likeness of Jesus Christ. In fact, conformity to Jesus Christ is one of God's key goals for us!

Think about God's goal of conforming us to the likeness of Christ. You may be wondering what having this goal would mean to you. I believe that this goal means that God's desire for you is that when you go to bed each night, you are a little more like Jesus than when you woke up that morning. You move toward this goal as you make knowing Jesus, loving Jesus, and serving Jesus the top priority of your day. When you make knowing, loving, and serving Jesus your top priority, you will experience freedom because you will experience Jesus! Why? Freedom is Christ—Christ in you!

In order to accomplish God's goal of conformity to the likeness of Christ, we must dispel the Wonder Woman mentality because it stands in the way of freedom. The Wonder Woman life calls us to live out of our own strength and power as we swoop from one problem to the next trying to conquer the world. This leaves us focused on earthly goals that can be accomplished in human power or strength. In order to be free, we must forsake a life that is focused solely on earthly things and embrace a life of conformity to Jesus Christ. This requires a willingness to surrender to God. As we surrender, we lay aside the Wonder Woman role and embrace the role of being Christ's servant. Then we are conformed to the likeness of Jesus and experience freedom in our daily life!

Think About It

Have you fallen into the trap of living your life based on the Wonder Woman mentality, swooping from one problem to the next trying your best to conquer the world? If so, how? _____

_____

_____

_____

_____

Please explain how the Wonder Woman mentality gets in the way of God's goal of conformity to Jesus Christ in your daily life. _____

_____

_____

_____

_____

Does the concept of knowing, loving, and serving Jesus more each day challenge you? Why or why not? _____

_____

_____

_____

_____

Respond To It

Close with a prayer committing to forsake the Wonder Woman mentality and embrace a life that is committed to conformity to the likeness of Jesus Christ.

_____

_____

_____

_____

_____

_____

Day 5:
A Willingness to be Rejected

> *"So they shook the dust from their feet in protest against them and went to Iconium. And the disciples were filled with joy and with the Holy Spirit."*
>
> *Acts 13:51–52*

Read It

Acts 13:51–52 will not make sense to you unless you understand the context of the passage. These two verses of Scripture hold a principle that helps us understand God's definition of freedom: godly freedom willingly accepts rejection. This is often a hard concept for women to accept. In general, women are pleasers. Women love to be loved and accepted. Women often go to great lengths to try to make everyone happy and maintain peace. They want to avoid the emotional pain that comes from rejection!

In Acts 13, the disciples of Jesus Christ took a different approach to rejection. The disciples learned early in their ministries that living for the name of Jesus Christ would produce rejection in their lives. The disciples embraced this truth and, as a result, experienced the freedom to be rejected without taking the rejection personally.

We see the freedom to be rejected firsthand in the Acts 13 account. Paul and Barnabas set out on their first missionary journey and traveled to a place called Pisidian Antioch. Once there, they spoke in the Jewish synagogue. Paul shared God's story of redemption, tracing the story from the time of Israel's slavery in Egypt to the time of Jesus' resurrection from the dead. Initially, Paul and Barnabas were accepted, and they were invited to speak again the following week. The next week the entire town arrived to hear the message Paul brought. The Jewish leaders became enraged with jealousy. Paul and Barnabas then turned to the Gentiles and shared the gospel message; many Gentiles believed. Scripture indicates that the word of the Lord spread throughout the region. The Jews did not like that people were coming to faith in Christ. As a result, the Jews incited prominent men and women to persecute Paul and Barnabas. In the end, the two apostles were expelled from the region.

If you are wondering how Paul and Barnabas handled this rejection, read today's passage. They shook the dust from their feet (which was a way of showing the town that the apostles would not be held responsible for the Jews in the town rejecting Christ) and headed to the next town with joy in their hearts. How could Paul and Barnabas respond to rejection in this way? They recognized that the rejection was not personal. The Jewish leaders were not rejecting the apostles—they were rejecting Christ!

Freedom came in Paul and Barnabas' lives when they embraced the truth that following Jesus would cost them. It would cost them their reputation. It would cost them their comfort. And in the end, it would cost them their lives. Although the cost was great, the reward was even greater. The reward became freedom to thrive on this earth as they lived a passionate life for Jesus Christ no matter the cost!

Today, do you need to hear that it is okay to be rejected for Jesus' sake? If so, look to God's Word and allow His Word to set you free. You can be rejected and still thrive. You can shake the dust off your feet and move on to the next stage in your life. You can experience rejection and still have a heart that is filled with joy and the Holy Spirit. The choice you face is this—will you accept the rejection that comes from living for Jesus Christ or will you give in to the voices around you telling you to live for acceptance in this world? May I encourage you to experience a little rejection? Then, shake the dust off your feet and move on!

Think About It

Please describe the areas of life where you need to take a stand even if that stand brings rejection. _____

_____

_____

_____

_____

_____

What scares you most about rejection? _____

_____

_____

_____

_____

_____

Do you see how the fear of rejection keeps you in bondage? _____

_____

_____

_____

_____

_____

Describe the freedom you will experience once you accept that following Christ may bring rejection into your life. _____

_____

_____

_____

_____

_____

Respond To It

Please journal a prayer asking the Lord to help you embrace rejection so that you can experience His freedom. _____

_____

_____

_____

_____

_____

_____

_____

Week 2:
A Serious View of Sin

*"We are free to thrive when we view
sin through the eyes of a holy God."*

Day 6:
A Serious View of Sin

"The vision of your prophets were false and worthless;
they did not expose your sin to ward off your captivity."

Lamentations 2:14

Read It

Sin. Just the mention of the word should make the believer's skin crawl. As believers, we should hate sin. We should hate the effect sin has on our lives. Unfortunately, we do not always hate sin. No. Sometimes we fail to view sin from God's holy perspective. Instead we choose to view it from a human perspective by allowing it to produce a thrill inside us. When we view sin as fun, exciting, thrilling, fulfilling, or acceptable, we are in a very dangerous situation.

The effect of sin in anyone's life is serious. For the unbeliever, sin separates that person from God and destines her to spend eternity away from God paying the penalty for her sin. For the believer, sin gets in the way of knowing, loving, and serving Jesus. Thus, sin inhibits the believer's walk with God and compromises her freedom in Jesus Christ.

The Old Testament details the effect sin had on the nation of Israel. In summary, sin led to captivity. Often the Israelites looked to false prophets instead of God's true prophets because the false prophets told them what they wanted to hear instead of what they needed to know. The inability of the false prophets to share truth and the lack of spiritual sensitivity on the part of the people to follow God with a whole heart, produced a level of comfort in God's people when it came to sin in their daily lives. This comfort led the Israelites to conceal their sin rather than expose it.

Just like the Old Testament false prophets led the people to conceal sin, we can fall into the same trap of concealing sin in our life. This occurs anytime sin produces a feeling of fun, excitement, thrill, fulfillment, or acceptance inside of us. The result of concealing sin is captivity to that sin. We attempt to conceal our sin when we justify sinful actions by saying:

- "It's not really that bad."
- "I will just do it this one time."
- "Everyone else is doing it."
- "It's how I was raised."
- "Compared to _____, I am not that bad."
- "I am not hurting anyone, so it does not really matter."

If you use one or more of these excuses to justify sin in your life, you can know that you are concealing sin and are not walking in spiritual freedom.

Freedom requires that we deal with sin every single day by committing to hate and expose every sin in our lives. I often pray this prayer to expose sin in my life: "Lord, shine Your bright light into every dark corner of my soul. Please expose the sin hidden in my life." I pray this prayer anytime I sense unconfessed sin in my heart. I then wait and watch for God to reveal the hidden areas of sin in me. I can assure you—God answers this prayer! God longs for us to walk in the freedom He provides; this walk will require that we have a proper view of sin.

Today, do you have a proper view of sin? Do you daily take on the job of exposing your sin rather than concealing it? If so, you are walking in freedom. If not, your vision for life is false and worthless, and you are living in captivity. Just like the Israelites faced physical captivity because they did not deal with the sin in their lives, believers face spiritual captivity anytime we chose to forsake a serious view of sin. Ask God to expose the sin in your life so that you can walk in the freedom He provides!

Think About It

Do you conceal or expose sin in your daily life? _____

_____

_____

_____

_____

Have you used one of the excuses listed in today's devotion to justify sin? If so, which one(s)? _____

_____

_____

_____

_____

Are there sinful thoughts or actions that you use in order to produce a sense of fun, excitement, thrill, fulfillment, or acceptance? If so, list the sins. (If you are not comfortable listing the sins on paper, speak them out loud to God.) Remember, the Bible says to confess your sins. Be specific. You cannot overcome what you do not recognize. _____

_____

_____

_____

_____

How do these sins keep you bound up in captivity instead of walking in freedom?

_____

_____

_____

Respond To It

Please journal a prayer asking the Lord to expose the sin in your life. Feel free to pray the same prayer I use. "Lord, shine Your bright light into every dark corner of my soul. Please expose the sin hidden in my heart!" _____

_____

_____

_____

_____

Day 7:
A Clean Thought Life

"We demolish arguments and every pretension that sets itself up against the knowledge of God, and we take captive every thought to make it obedient to Christ."

2 Corinthians 10:5

Read It

Getting real about sin involves examining our thought processes. We need to ask questions like: "What do I think about on a daily basis, and how are these thoughts leading me to be more like Christ?" It is easy to overlook our thought processes because we often give little consideration to the constant stream of thoughts flowing through our hearts and minds. Without a doubt, we must examine our thought lives. The things we think about impact the way we act and the way we feel.

The apostle Paul recognized the importance of a clean thought life. In 2 Corinthians 10:5, Paul provided two instructions for achieving and maintaining such a life.

1. **Demolish:** The first step to a clean thought life is demolishing. Here are the key terms.
   - Demolish: This word means to crush or destroy.
   - Arguments: This word means reflections or considerations; in some translations, it is rendered as imaginations.
   - Pretension: This word gives the idea of an aspiration that has yet to be reached.

A good summary of Paul's instructions would be: "Destroy or crush reflections, considerations, imaginations, or aspirations in your life that are false according to God's standard of truth."

2. **Take captive:** The second step to a clean though life involves taking captive, which involves one essential step.

   • Take captive: This phrase means to overcome or overpower.

A good summary of Paul's instruction would be: "Overcome or overpower every thought that goes on in your heart and mind, and make your thoughts obedient to Jesus Christ."

Wow! What an overwhelming but important task we face! If we do not demolish and take captive impure thoughts, our minds will become a cesspool for sin, resulting in an unfiltered, contaminated mind.

An unfiltered mind is a dangerous trap that always leads to captivity. An unfiltered mind provides countless hours of daydreaming, imagining, and wondering about a secret life that is not our own. Our daydreams might involve a different spouse, a different career, an unfulfilled dream, a different set of circumstances, or an unresolved issue from our past.

We are free when we regularly demolish and take captive these thoughts and make them obedient to Jesus Christ. In a sense, we turn on the filter of Jesus Christ and allow Him to say what thoughts can stay and what thoughts must go! Demolishing and taking captive is a life-long process. We will never be able to check this one off our lists. As we demolish and take captive our thoughts, we will experience freedom as we get rid of wrong thoughts and replace them with right thoughts.

In order to take every thought captive to Jesus Christ, the Word of God plays a vital role. The Bible provides the standard by which we measure which thoughts can stay in our minds and which thoughts must go! Today, examine your thoughts. Have you allowed some thoughts in your mind that simply need to go?

Think About It

Do you daydream, imagine, or wonder about a life that is not your present reality?

_____

_____

_____

Please explain how daydreaming, imagining, or wondering compromises your spiritual freedom. _____

_____

_____

_____

_____

What will it take for you to demolish and take captive these thoughts to make them obedient to Jesus Christ?_____

_____

_____

_____

How does the concept of a spiritual filter help you determine which thoughts can stay in your mind and which thoughts must go? _____

_____

_____

_____

Respond To It

Please journal a prayer asking the Lord to make your stomach sick every time you try to escape your real life and hide in a secret one._____

_____

_____

_____

_____

_____

Day 8:
A Tamed Tongue

"Set a guard over my mouth, O Lord;
keep watch over the door of my lips."

Psalm 141:3

Read It

How often do our lips get us in trouble? Have you ever walked away from a conversation and asked yourself, "Why did I say that?" I will confess that I have! Anytime I find my lips getting me in trouble, I breathe a quick prayer asking the Lord to guard my mouth and watch over my lips.

Words are powerful—not because they hold power in and of themselves but because they reveal the state of our hearts. Jesus said, "But the things that come out of a person's mouth come from the heart…"(Matthew 15:18). This truth makes words very powerful.

There are so many ways we can sin with our mouths. Critical words, harsh words, gossip, exaggeration, foul words, and words meant to put someone in their place are just a few examples. These types of words are not in line with God's desires for our lives and often become a form of self-preservation.

Each day we need to evaluate our words by examining the way we talk to our husbands, children, friends, co-workers, and even ourselves. Any time we sin with our mouths, we should stop and confess the sin to God. Once we have confessed the sin, we also need to go to the person we sinned against and ask for their forgiveness.

Not long ago, I was on the phone with a friend. I was telling a story and exaggerated some of the details. After I hung up the phone, I sensed the Lord's conviction. I knew that I needed to pick up the phone and on call my friend back. My friend was gracious as I apologized for exaggerating the details of the story. I will be honest with you that I was embarrassed by my actions. However, making that second phone call was the best thing for me to do. Since that time, I have thought twice before exaggerating a story!

We are free to thrive when we speak God's words, not our own. This requires discipline and a sensitive spirit. When we recognize that we are going into a potentially dangerous conversation (one that easily could lead us to sin with our mouths), we need to be on guard and bathe that conversation in prayer. As we pray, we can ask the Lord to stop us when we begin to journey down a dangerous path. Then, when we are in the middle of the conversation, we can display a sensitive spirit by listening to the Holy Spirit. When we sense conviction over the direction of our conversation, we can stop the conversation immediately.

For just a moment, imagine NOT walking away from a conversation saying, "Why did I say that?" Instead you walk away from a conversation with a sense of peace in your heart—a peace that results from knowing that God's words flowed from your mouth as you made the choice to invite Him to set a guard over your mouth and to keep watch over your lips. Now that is freedom!

Think About It

Explain your greatest struggle when it comes to the words that flow from your mouth. Do you struggle with using critical words, harsh words, gossip, exaggeration, foul words, or words that are meant to put someone in his or her place? _____

_____

_____

_____

Explain how this behavior leads to bondage instead of freedom. _____

_____

_____

_____

Are you willing to be disciplined and sensitive in this area of your life by asking the Lord to set a guard over your mouth and to keep watch over your lips?   Yes   No

Do you need to confess to people in your life and tell them you sinned against them with your words?   Yes   No

If yes, how and when will you take this step of obedience? _____

_____

_____

_____

Respond To It

Please journal a prayer asking the Lord to help you embrace freedom by speaking His words and not your own. _____

_____

_____

_____

_____

_____

Day 9:
A Christ-honoring Temple

> *"Do you not know that your body is a temple of the Holy Spirit, who is in you, whom you have received from God? You are not your own; you were bought at a price. Therefore honor God with your body."*
>
> *1 Corinthians 6:19-20*

Read It

Freedom requires that we view our physical bodies as the dwelling place of the Holy Spirit. This means that we understand that our bodies provide a physical home for the eternal God. Therefore every action that goes on in our bodies or through our bodies determines if our bodies provides a Christ-honoring temple for the Spirit of God to dwell in.

Nothing displeases God more than sin. All sin occurs in and through the body. Vicious sin cycles—sins that occur over and over again to the point were we think there is little hope for change—occur via the body. A few examples are cutting, drinking, binging/purging, overeating, smoking, addiction, sexual misbehavior, stealing, and the like. Everyone struggles with some form of sin, even though many believers give the impression that they don't. Freedom comes in getting real and getting rid of the sin that takes place in and through our bodies. The getting real and getting rid process is a hard process that requires honesty with ourselves and honesty with our loving heavenly Father. We must identify the sin in our lives so that we can take the necessary steps to get rid of that sin.

The first step to getting real and getting rid of sin in our lives is recognizing that our bodies do not belong to us. At the moment of our salvation, the Holy Spirit entered our hearts, and our bodies became His dwelling place. Therefore, we are guests in someone else's home. When we think about the way we act in someone else's home, we quickly understand the truth Paul taught—that we need to pay close attention to the behavior that takes place in and through our bodies. When I take my kids to someone else's home I often tell them, "You are a guest—be on your best behavior." In mom-talk this means "Be extra careful, do not mess up, and make your mom proud." Paul communicated the same desire when he asked the question, "Do you not know that your body is a temple of the Holy Spirit, who is in you, whom you have received from God?" Then Paul made this statement, "You are not your own…." In short, Paul communicated our need to be extra careful. We need to strive to avoid a mess up. We need to make God proud.

The second step to getting real and getting rid of the sin in our lives is understanding the price that was paid for our freedom. Paul reminds us, "You were bought at a price." The price for our freedom was Jesus' perfect sinless body. This truth is stated in 1 Peter 2:24. "(Jesus) himself bore our sins in his body on the tree, so that we might die to sins and live for righteousness; by his wounds you have been healed." On the cross, Jesus bore the punishment for the sins we commit. Because God is holy, He cannot be in the presence of sin. Therefore, a price had to be paid. The price was Jesus' life. While on the cross, Jesus endured God's wrath towards sin. He became our substitute. We should have died, but Jesus died in our place. Jesus' death satisfied God's wrath towards sin and provided a way for you and me to know God personally. Recognizing this important truth puts sin into a proper perspective. Sin is serious because it cost Jesus His life. Through Jesus' death, burial, and resurrection, freedom has been provided for every sin we now face.

The third step to getting real and getting rid of the sin in our lives is surrendering to the call to honor God with every part of our bodies. In verse 20, Paul states, "Honor God with your body." The word honor means to recognize: this concept provides a clear path to breaking those sin cycles. Every day we need to wake up and use our hands, feet, arms, legs, mouth, mind, and heart to recognize the Lord. As we do, our bodies becomes a dwelling or resting place that is honoring to the Lord

We are free to thrive when sin cycles that take place in our bodies are broken in Jesus' name. When this occurs we can know that the Lord is right at home in us and that our bodies provide a Christ-honoring place for Him to dwell. Today, remember that your body is not your own and you were bought with a price. So honor God with every part of your body!

Think About It

Do you engage in a sin cycle with your body that displeases the Lord? If so, please describe. _____

_____

_____

_____

_____

As a result of the sin cycle, do you live a defeated life? _____

_____

_____

_____

_____

Of the three steps listed in today's study (recognize that your body does not belong to you, understand the price that was paid for your sin, and surrender to the call to honor God with every part of your body), which challenges you the most and why?

_____

_____

_____

_____

Today, how will you incorporate these truths into your life? _____

_____

_____

_____

_____

Respond To It

You are free to thrive when you get real and get rid of sin in your life. Please journal a prayer asking the Lord to provide freedom as you turn from sin and recognize that your body is not your own._____

_____

_____

_____

_____

Day 10:
A Christ-centered Approval Process

"Am I now trying to win the approval of men,
or of God? Or am I trying to please men? If I were still
trying to please men, I would not be a servant of Christ."

Galatians 1:10

Read It

People-pleasing! It is epidemic among women. No matter what a woman's age, background, or social standing is, she longs to be loved and accepted by others. While this desire is natural, it becomes sin when the desire controls a woman's life. People-pleasing inhibits freedom because it keeps us bound up trying to please others instead of Christ.

In Galatians 1:10, Paul draws a clear line in the sand. The primary focus for the believer should be pleasing Christ, not others. Paul provides his life as an example. His life demonstrates how we should live lives that reflect a Christ-centered approval process. I must admit that Galatians 1:10 is near and dear to my heart. This is true because I have struggled with people-pleasing most of my life.

As a pleaser, I wanted everyone to like me and affirm the direction of my life. This desire resulted in an unhealthy behavior pattern. When it came time to make a decision, I went to others for direction. Instead of filtering their advice through God's Word, I found myself trapped by all the advice I received. I thought I had to follow every piece of advice or risk hurting someone's feelings. This trap felt so tangible that it often produced feelings of anxiety inside of me. Little did I know that I was being controlled by the desires of other people. Thus, I was striving to please others instead of striving to please Christ.

Often the people we long to please are close to our hearts—our parents, spouse, friends, coworkers, children, church leaders, or boss. When our desire to please Christ supersedes our desire to please those around us, we have a healthier perspective.

If you struggle with an unhealthy desire to please others instead of Christ, consider taking the following steps.

- Stop seeking advice from others. Take a break from asking other people what you should do in life. Instead, use your time to talk to God.
- Saturate yourself in God's Holy Word. Know His Word and allow the Bible to guide your decisions.
- Surround yourself with godly people who will hold you accountable on this important issue. Share your struggle of people-pleasing with a close friend or family member. Be honest with them and let them know you long for freedom in this area of life. When you go to them for advice, encourage them to ask, "Have

you prayed about this?" or, "What does God's Word have to say?" If you have not prayed about the decision, or if you do not know what the Bible has to say, stop talking to others and start praying.

I promise you there is nothing like freedom in this area of life. As you allow the Word of God to become your standard, clear instruction takes the place of unclear opinions. The result? Your desire to please Christ will supersede your desire to please others. No longer will you be bound up by an ever-changing system of thought that is dictated by the desires of others. Rather, you will experience a desire to embrace Jesus' thoughts, plans, and desires for your life. The benefit of a Christ-centered approval process is fellowship with God. As you turn to the Lord and ask Him what you should do, you will experience a close fellowship with the Lord as He becomes your best friend. Dear friend, if you are caught in the trap of people-pleasing, know that freedom is available today!

Think About It

In all honesty, whom do you strive to please more—people or God? _____
_____
_____
_____

Do you value people's opinions over God's opinion? Yes   No

If so, please explain how this tendency compromises spiritual freedom in your life.
_____
_____
_____

Which of the tangible steps listed in today's devotion is God calling you to embrace? Are you willing? _____
_____
_____
_____

Respond To It

Please journal a prayer asking the Lord to help you seek His approval, not others'.
_____
_____
_____
_____
_____

Week 3:
A Proper View of God's Word

*"We are free to thrive when
we heed the words of Christ."*

Day 11:
A Love for God's Word

"If you hold to my teaching, you are really my disciples. Then you will know the truth, and the truth will set you free."

John 8:31–32

Read It

We all know what it is like to want freedom. We long for freedom. We ask for freedom. Yet, we often fail to do the one thing that leads to freedom! Jesus said freedom comes as you hold to His teachings. I love the simplicity of this verse. Jesus did not give ten steps to freedom—He gave one! In essence He said, "If you want freedom, follow My living, breathing, and always sufficient Word." Following Jesus' Word involves two steps—knowing His Word and obeying His Word.

1. Do you know His Word?

The teachings recorded in the Bible provide freedom because they express the heart of God on big and small issues of life. Knowing the Word of God occurs as we daily interact with the Bible. Our daily interaction must be personal. We must know the Bible so well that even when the Bible is not in front of us, the truths of the Bible ring in our hearts. May I ask you a personal question? How much of God's holy Word do you have access to in your heart? God has given His Word to be a source of light in a very dark world. Believers must take the light and allow it to shine bright in their lives. This occurs as we read God's Word and allow it to change the way we live.

2. Do you hold to the teachings in His Word?

Jesus said, "If you hold to my teachings, you are really my disciples." Think about this. In order to hold onto an object, we must make the choice to grab the object, and we must display an active determination not to let go of the object. Holding on to Jesus' teachings occurs in the same way. First, we must daily make the choice to grab His holy thoughts regarding our lives by choosing to spend time with God the Father. Second, we must display an active determination to hold on to His thoughts by allowing them to change the way we live on a very practical level. This means the teachings found in the Bible must impact the way we interact with our husband, children, co-workers, and friends. As we hold on to Jesus' teachings, freedom flows into our lives and through our lives as we learn to live by standards set forth in His Holy Word.

We are free to thrive as we seek God's direction in His holy Word and surrender to that direction, no matter the cost. Today, I challenge you to grab on to Jesus' teachings and hold on to them!

Think About It

How often do you turn to God's Word for direction in your daily life? _____

_____

_____

_____

How diligent are you to hold on to the teachings found in God's Word as you live each day? _____

_____

_____

List an area(s) in your life where you need to grab on to Jesus' teachings and hold on to them in your daily life. _____

_____

_____

_____

How would it change your life if you followed God's instructions in these areas of life?

_____

_____

_____

Do you see how following the Bible would produce freedom in your life? If so, please explain. _____

_____

_____

_____

Respond To It

Please journal a prayer asking the Lord to help you embrace freedom by knowing His truth and allowing His truth to set you free. _____

_____

_____

_____

_____

_____

_____

Day 12:
An Enduring Hope

> *"For everything that was written in the past was written to teach us, so that through endurance and the encouragement of the Scriptures we might have hope."*
>
> *Romans 15:4*

Read It

Let's get straight to the point. Where do you find your hope? Paul stated his source of hope in Romans 15:4. Paul's hope came from the teachings found in God's Word.

God's Word provides hope because it tells the story of God. From Genesis to Revelation, we read the epic story of God, unfolding one page at a time. Here is a brief overview of God's story:

1. Creation of man (Genesis 1)
2. Fall of man (Genesis 3)
3. Noah and the flood (Genesis 5)
4. Call of Abram (Genesis 12)
5. Covenant with Abraham (Genesis 15)
6. Joseph sold into slavery and later promoted to leadership in Egypt (Genesis 37–50)
7. Deliverance of God's people from Egyptian slavery (Exodus 1–12)
8. Giving of the Ten Commandments (Exodus 20)
9. Rebellion of God's people (the Israelites) in the desert (Exodus 32 and Numbers 13–14)
10. Entrance of the new generation of Israelites into the Promised Land (Deuteronomy and Joshua)
11. Struggle of God's people to follow God's instructions once in the Promised Land. (Judges to 2 Chronicles)
12. Rebellion of God's people and subsequent punishment from God in the form of exile to Babylonian captivity. (2 Kings)
13. Rebuilding Jerusalem following Babylonian captivity (Ezra and Nehemiah)
14. Ministry of the prophets foretelling the coming of the Messiah. (Isaiah to Malachi)
15. Birth of Jesus (the Gospels)
16. Life and ministry of Jesus (the Gospels)
17. Death, burial, resurrection, and ascension of Jesus (the Gospels)

18. Development of the early Church, including the Gentiles being grafted in to God's family (Acts and the New Testament letters)

19. Life and ministry of Paul and the other apostles as the name of Jesus spread to the then-known world. (Acts and the New Testament letters)

20. Writing of Revelation describing the future moment when Jesus will return to establish the new heaven and the new earth—when there will be no more tears, no more pain, and no more death. Finally, believers in Jesus Christ will live in perfect fellowship with God the Father. (Revelation)

While this summary is concise, it accurately portrays the over-arching story of God—a story that began before Creation and has no end. Through the reading of God's story, one thing is clear. God has a plan. This truth should provide hope in our daily lives as it teaches us how to live our lives with God's perspective. God's perspective reminds us that His Word was written thousands of years ago in order to capture and chronicle His epic story. God graciously preserved this story through oral tradition and later written word so that thousands of years later we can live our lives based on truth. Isn't that an amazing thought? God in His infinite wisdom knew that we would need clear instruction as well as a God-size picture of His work on this earth so that we can have an enduring source of hope in our lives. As a result, God preserved His Word for you and me!

It is easy to fall into the trap of allowing things like our career, husband, children, paycheck, health status, or social standing to provide a sense of hope in our daily lives. However, the truth is these areas cannot produce long-term hope because any one of them can change in an instant. Hope comes as we know the Word and allow the Word to teach us how to live based on God's eternal perspective. King David recognized this truth when he wrote Psalm 130:5, "In his word I put my hope." So here's the question for you: "Where do you put your hope? In the world or in the Word?"

Think About It

Do you fall into the trap of trying to find your hope in the situations of life like your career, family, health status, or social standing? _____

_____

_____

_____

How would your life change if you viewed God's Word as your source of enduring hope? _____

_____

_____

_____

_____

_____

Please explain the importance of viewing your life from God's eternal perspective as seen in the story of God as it unfolds through the Word. _____

_____

_____

_____

Respond To It

Please journal a prayer asking God to grant you a love for His Word and an ability to view His Word as your source of hope in life. _____

_____

_____

_____

_____

_____

Day 13:
A Sanctifying Source

> *"Now I commit you to God and to the word of grace, which can build you up and give you an inheritance among all those who are sanctified."*
>
> *Acts 20:32*

Read It

Today I want to share a word with you that is exciting and life-changing. Chances are you have heard this word before. I heard this word a lot as I was growing up, but I never really understood its meaning. Perhaps, like me, you heard this word but didn't really grasp what it meant. This word is sanctified.

I love the word sanctified because it communicates an important biblical concept. Sanctified communicates the biblical call of being set apart from the world and daily growing in our love and devotion for Jesus Christ. In essence, the woman who is sanctified or surrendering to the sanctifying process is becoming more like Jesus and less like the world every single day she lives on this earth.

Acts 20:32 communicates the importance of the sanctification process. In this passage, Paul spoke to a group of beloved church leaders before he departed for Jerusalem where he would face hardship, trials, and imprisonment. Luke recorded Paul's words and God preserved Paul's words through the Bible. Paul said, "Now I commit you to God and to the word of grace, which can build you up and give you an inheritance among all those who are sanctified." This verse highlights the truth that Paul committed the people that he loved to God and to the word of grace, which we have in the form of the Bible. Further Paul shared that the word of grace can build up our lives and give us a reward among the people who are sanctified—becoming more like Jesus and less like the world.

For you and me, God's Word is our sanctifying source. God's Word contains clear instruction for how we should live and must be the source we access if we are going to live lives that are sanctified or set apart in Christ. I love the mental picture I receive when I think about the Bible building up my life. Step by step, the Bible moves me closer towards my real home. Do you sense the forward progression in this thought? I do.

For a moment, consider the building-up process—the process of sanctification being worked out in our daily lives. Building up requires focus and direction for us to become more like Christ and less like the world. Thus, building up nullifies building for the sake of building alone. This means building up keeps us from living a life with no real sense of direction or clear-cut goals. Building up has one goal in mind, and that is the goal of becoming more like Jesus in the way we think, act, and feel. Building up also nullifies the thought of not building at all as seen in living our lives with no focus or too much focus on the past rather than the future. Too often women live with the weight of their past causing them to lose focus. This happens each time a woman spends more time thinking about "what might have been" rather than "what really is!" Finally, building up nullifies living with the horizontal focus of living for the things of this world. Rather, it calls us to place our eyes on the prize of our heavenly home.

Certainly, the Bible is our "how to" guide for sanctification. The Bible teaches us how to become more like Christ as we forsake the things of this world. Thus, as we surrender to the teachings found in the Bible, our lives are built up in Christ. Daily interacting with the Word of God will provide us with an inheritance that we will never lose. As we interact with the Bible, we become more like Christ in the way we live. The outcome of this process will be a heavenly reward of God's affirmation regarding the way we lived our lives while on earth. I don't know about you, but I do not want to miss out on a heavenly reward. So today's question is, "Are you being sanctified by God's Word?

Think About It

Are you building up (becoming more like Christ), not building at all (living with no focus or too much focus on the past), or building horizontally (focused on the things of this world) in your daily life? _____

_____

_____

_____

_____

_____

How can building up (becoming more like Christ) lead to freedom?_____

_____

_____

_____

_____

Describe your daily interaction with the Bible. _____

_____

_____

_____

_____

What is God calling you to do to increase your time or effectiveness in His Word?

_____

_____

_____

_____

Respond To It

Journal a prayer asking the Lord to grant you a love for His word as you live your life sanctified in Him._____

_____

_____

_____

_____

_____

_____

Day 14:
A Deadly Weapon

*"Set me free from my prison, that I may praise
your name. Then the righteous will gather
about me because of your goodness to me."*

Psalm 142:7

Read It

God's Word can and should be used as a deadly weapon in our lives. The apostle Paul described the Word of God as the sword of the Spirit in Ephesians 6:17. I love this picture of God's Word being used as a sword. In my daily life, I need a sharp weapon to cut through and cut out the sin that impacts my life. We all do!

In the psalm quoted above, David spoke of a time when he was forced to hide in a cave from King Saul. Though we do not know if David was referring to a literal or figurative prison as he asked God for deliverance, we do know that David longed for freedom in his life.

We should long for freedom in our lives too, both literally and figuratively. Spiritual "prisons" come in many different forms. Often spiritual prisons fall into one of the following categories:

- An unknown fear
- A vicious sin cycle
- A nagging past.

Prisons like these keep women lying awake at night wondering: "What will happen next?" "Will I ever be free?" "Can God use someone like me?"

The thing I hate most about spiritual prisons is that they keep believers bound up and focused on their own concerns. Have you ever noticed that before? Spiritual prisons cause us to spend more time thinking about what we have done or what we need rather than the Lord and His desires for our lives.

David recognized this tendency as he wrote Psalm 142:7. Note the reason David wanted to be free from his spiritual prison—"that I may praise your name." David knew his prison was keeping him from fully praising the name of the Lord. Therefore, David wanted freedom so that nothing would stand in the way of his ability to worship God with every part of his being. What a great perspective to have in life!

If you and I gain the same perspective as David, we too will begin to hate our spiritual prisons. As a result, we will begin to fight for freedom because our spiritual prisons keep us from fully and completely praising the Lord. I don't know about you, but that makes me want to get up and fight!

Today, do you need to fight to be free from some spiritual prisons in your life? If so, begin by getting a vision of freedom. Imagine your life free from the chains that currently bind you. Next, fight with all your might. Use the Word of God, which is your sword, and fight, fight, fight. Find passages of scripture that speak directly to the prison you currently face. Once you find a passage, memorize it. Say the passage over and over again. Write the passage on a note card and carry it with you. Tape the passage to your mirror, refrigerator door, or the rearview mirror in your car. Whatever you do, fight well armed with God's holy Word. Know that freedom can come in your life as you surrender to God's Word and fight with all your God-given might!

Think About It

List your spiritual prison(s)—areas of fear, vicious sin cycles, or issues from your the past.

_____

_____

_____

List a passage of scripture that speaks to each prison. If necessary, search by topic using your Bible concordance or an on-line Bible search tool. _____

_____

_____

_____

Develop a plan. How are you going to fight well armed with God's Word?

- _____
- _____
- _____
- _____
- _____

Respond To It

Journal a prayer asking the Lord help you apply His Word as you fight for spiritual freedom in your daily life!_____

_____

_____

_____

_____

_____

Day 15:
A Determination to Seek

"My eyes are ever on the Lord, for only he will release my feet from the snare."

Psalm 25:15

Read It

I remember a time when I lost my son in a busy fast-food restaurant. In just seconds, I went from being a customer having a casual lunch to being a determined mother who would stop at nothing in order to find her boy. My determination caught the attention of others as they left their tables and began to look. The two minutes that Andrew was missing seemed like an eternity. As the seconds ticked by, my desire to find Andrew grew stronger and stronger. Thankfully, I found Andrew, and he does not even remember the event. I can assure you, I do!

The opening phrase of Psalm 25:15 challenges us in our seeking process. It states, "My eyes are ever on the Lord." In this statement, David determined to look to the Lord in his daily walk. The words, "are ever on," communicated his commitment to the seeking process. David would not embrace a casual approach to seeking. Instead, he would seek the Lord much like I sought my lost son—with determination!

David's seeking process brought deliverance. The last half of Psalm 25:15 states, "for only he will release my feet from the snare." As David diligently sought the Lord, he was delivered from the snares of his life.

Each day we face snares—situations and circumstances that invite us to look away from the Lord. In response, we must determine to fix our eyes on the Lord. One way to measure our spiritual focus is by asking the question, "Do I glance or do I gaze?"

- **Glance:** to take a quick look, to catch a glimpse, to touch on a subject briefly or indirectly.
- **Gaze:** to fix the eyes in a steady intent, to look often with eagerness and studious attention.

Gazing involves determination to seek the Lord on crazy days as well as calm ones. Consistent gazing produces deliverance in our homes and in our lives. Today, I challenge you to make the choice to move past a mere glance at the Lord and embrace a gaze. Don't let anything stop you!

Think About It

What situation(s) draw your attention away from gazing at the Lord?_____

_____

_____

_____

What role should God's Word play in your gazing process?_____

_____

_____

_____

Respond To It

Today I want to challenge you to gaze on God, no matter what! Here are a few practical ways that you can gaze:

- Incorporate praise and worship music into your day by listening to songs of praise during your daily routine. I like to listen to praise and worship music first thing in the morning as I get ready for my day and last thing before I go to bed.
- Memorize Psalm 25:15. Write the verse on a notecard and carry it with you throughout your day. Find the wasted two and three minutes in your day and focus on hiding God's word in your heart.
- Actively look for a way to help someone in need. As you focus on others, God will show you how He is at work around you. This action will help you to gaze at God.

Which tip are you going to incorporate into your day? _____

_____

_____

How will this action help you to gaze at God? _____

_____

_____

_____

Please journal a prayer asking the Lord to help you be determined to gaze on Him in your life._____

_____

_____

_____

_____

Week 4:
A Right Theology

"We are free to thrive when we base our lives on correct theology."

Day 16:
A Biblically Grounded Life

*"I am the light of the world. Whoever follows me will
never walk in darkness, but will have the light of life."*

John 8:12

Read It

When I was in high school, I regularly walked or jogged in my neighborhood late at night. Although I lived in a close-knit community, I often became nervous when I heard a sound or saw a shadow. To remain calm, I focused my attention completely on the glowing streetlights. As I focused on the light, the darkness no longer affected me.

In John 8:12, Jesus communicated a simple truth: Focus on the light. Who is the light? Jesus is the light. As we focus on Jesus, we learn how to live amidst the darkness of this world that believes there is no absolute truth. It's a world that promotes an anything-goes kind of life, a world that teaches us to serve ourselves.

As we walk in this dark world, we must live a biblically grounded life that is based on correct theology as stated in the Bible. Correct theology provides a concrete system of beliefs about who God is and the role He should play in our lives. When we embrace correct theology, we have a set of "go to" assurances that provide certainty during the darkest times.

The benefit of correct theology cannot be overstated. Correct theology provides truth. Truth provides direction. Direction provides practical steps. Practical steps lead to freedom as we recognize what the Bible says and allow the teachings of the Bible to impact the way we live on a daily basis. When we base our actions and attitudes on correct theology, we discover a source of peace, power, and strength that propels us through the darkness of this world towards the light of Jesus Christ.

This week we will see how correct theology frees us up to live a thriving life in Jesus Christ as we explore the following topics:

- God is our awesome creator. He gave us life.
- God is our powerful sustainer. He takes care of us.
- God is our plentiful provider. He gives us everything we need.
- God is our passionate protector. He knows the number of days we will spend on this earth and everything we will accomplish while on this earth.

In response to these truths, we can shout, "What can man do to me?" The answer is: "NOTHING!" For me, this truth provides freedom! God's Word is full of theology. From Genesis to Revelation, the Word records who God is and the role He longs to play in our lives. As we live our lives based on correct theology, we will be free to thrive as we live in the light of Jesus Christ.

Think About It

Do you need to broaden the scope of your biblical knowledge so that correct theology plays an active role in your life?_____

_____

_____

_____

Have you ever considered how a lack of biblical knowledge leads to spiritual bondage?
Yes   No

Please explain how a lack of biblical knowledge can lead to spiritual bondage in your life.

_____

_____

_____

Respond To It

Please journal a prayer asking the Lord to teach you correct biblical knowledge through His holy Word._____

_____

_____

_____

_____

_____

Day 17:
An Awesome Creator

> *"Be still, and know that I am God; I will be exalted among the nations, I will be exalted in the earth."*
>
> *Psalm 46:10*

Read It

As you read today's verse, I want you to do something different. I want to ask you to be still. That's right. No movement, just stillness before the Lord. Take a few minutes and allow your mind to clear away all the distractions of this world. Then think about this. You have a relationship with the Creator of the universe. Amazing, isn't it?

As you enjoy a moment of stillness before the Lord, focus on one important theological truth. God is God, and you are not. God is the Creator. He has always been in control, even before time began. Nothing takes the Creator by surprise. Nothing is beyond the Creator's ability to control.

We are the creation. God made us. He formed and fashioned us. Nothing about our lives is a surprise or an accident. The Creator we serve knows everything about us. He knows everything that has happened to us. No thought can come into our minds and no words can come out of our mouths without Him knowing it. Psalm 139:4 beautifully states this truth: "Before a word is on my tongue, you know it completely, O Lord."

God is our awesome Creator. Each day we need to take time and meditate on this truth. As we consider it, we recognize the fact that God is God and we are not. Surrendering to this theological truth places us in the position to be less worried about the things taking place during our day. As a result, a new discipline will develop in our daily walk with God. We will recognize that God is in control of every aspect of our life. God, our awesome Creator, is in control! There is nothing that we face when we wake up in the morning that God cannot handle. There is no worry too big that He cannot bear. When we go to sleep at night, we can rest easy, knowing that He has us in the palm of His hands.

Dear friend, God is your awesome Creator. No matter how out of control your life may feel, God is on His throne. In light of this truth, I want to invite you to daily rest in Him. As you rest, you will be free to thrive, knowing He is God and you are not.

Think About It

List the areas that keep you awake at night or worried during your day. _____

_____

_____

_____

_____

_____

In light of the above response, I invite you to view God as your awesome Creator. Please explain how this view of God will help you to live a free life in Christ.

_____

_____

_____

_____

_____

_____

Respond To It

Take a few minutes and journal a prayer to the Lord. Thank Him that you do not have to be God. Then, give Him every area of your life and rest in the fact that God, your awesome Creator, is on His throne. _____

_____

_____

_____

_____

Day 18:
A Powerful Sustainer

"I lie down and sleep; I wake again, because the Lord sustains me.
I will not fear the tens of thousands drawn up against me on every side."

Psalm 3:5–6

Read It

Imagine your son stealing your job, chasing you out of town, and pursuing you in order to take your life. These events describe the events surrounding David's life as he wrote Psalm 3:5–6. Absalom, David's son, rebelled against his father and assumed the role of king. Then Absalom devised a plan to kill David and pursued his father in order to carry out his plan.

In the midst of this difficult time, David reacted like any human being. He wondered how to respond. David worried about how things would turn out. He wept over the breakdown of his family and nation.

The storyline for these events in David's life is recorded in chapters 15 through 18 of 2 Samuel. The height of David's struggle with Absalom is recorded in 2 Samuel 15:14: "David said to his officials who were with him in Jerusalem, 'Come! We must flee, or none of us will escape from Absalom. We must leave immediately, or he will move quickly to overtake us and bring ruin upon us and put the city to the sword.'"

The situation looked bleak for David and his kingship. From a worldly standpoint, David was as good as dead, BUT God had a plan. God was in control, sustaining David through the entire situation. As Absalom pursued David in order to kill him, Absalom lost his own life. When his mule passed under a tree, Absalom's head was caught in the branches, exposing him to David's soldiers who killed him. David was once again the uncontested king of Israel. God sustained David by providing support to David and relief from Absalom's evil plan. God prolonged David's kingship and ultimately his life.

Prior to Absalom's death, David came to a place of peace regarding his own life. Even though David's life and kingship were as good as done from a worldly standpoint, he wrote these words: "I lie down and sleep; I wake again, because the Lord sustains me."

Profound theological truth is found in this short passage of scripture. God sustains your life. As a result, you can have great confidence as you live your life on this earth. God determines when you live and when you die. Without a doubt, evil exists in the world because we live in a world that is ravaged by sin. As a result, death, disease, and deplorable acts occur. We can know that God is not the author of these acts because God is pure, holy, and loving. However, God is sovereign over everything that happens in this world and to His children. Sin, death, and dismay are not stronger than our God! We serve a sustaining God, and at the sound of His voice everything can change.

What would it be like if you started living your life based on the truth that God sustains your life? For me, confidence would surface and fear would subside. Many women face challenging battles—health issues, difficult relationships, and turbulent life events that keep them questioning their future. "How should I respond to this event in my life?" "Will things ever be the same?" "Can my family recover?"

In the midst of these battles, we must know this truth—God sustains our life. Our lives are not in the power of anything or anyone stronger than our God. Our lives are in the hands of our loving Father! I love the last phrase of Psalm 3:6, "I will not fear the tens of thousands drawn up against me on every side." Can you relate? Do you know what it is like to face an obstacle that feels like tens of thousands of people are against you? If so, do not fear. Your life rests secure in the hands and heart of your sustaining God.

Today, do you need to hear the truth that God sustains your life? Are you facing a battle that leaves you wondering what will happen next? If so, take God's Word to heart—the Lord sustains your life. Allow freedom to take the place of fear as you experience God as your powerful Sustainer.

Think About It

Are you facing battles that leave you feeling vulnerable to physical, emotional, or mental harm? If so, please describe._____

_____

_____

_____

_____

Describe the fear that results from these battles. _____

_____

_____

_____

How does this fear compromise your spiritual freedom in Jesus Christ? _____

_____

_____

_____

Today, have you been confronted with the truth that God sustains your life? Does this truth provide freedom for you? If so, please describe. _____

_____

_____

_____

_____

_____

Respond To It

Please close by journaling a prayer asking the Lord to sustain your life by His powerful hand. _____

_____

_____

_____

_____

_____

_____

Day 19:
A Plentiful Provider

> *"The LORD answered Moses, 'Is the LORD's arm too short? You will now see whether or not what I say will come true for you.'"*
>
> *Numbers 11:23*

Read It

The context of today's verse is very important to understand. It will help us grasp the verse's depth of meaning. The Israelites were on their journey from Egypt to the promised land. They grew tired of eating manna, the bread-like substance God provided during their desert wandering experience. They longed for meat and other foods they ate during Egyptian captivity.

Moses heard the complaining in the camp and turned to the Lord to express his thoughts of frustration. Moses stated, "Why have you brought this trouble on your servant? What have I done to displease you that you put the burden of all these people on me? Did I conceive all these people? Did I give them birth? Why do you tell me to carry them in my arms, as a nurse carries an infant, to the land you promised on oath to their forefathers? Where can I get meat for all these people?" (Numbers 11:11–13).

Can you imagine the frustration in Moses's voice? I can. Moses was God's chosen servant to lead the nation of Israel out of Egypt and into the promised land. But there was a problem—the people were hard to lead! The Israelites often looked backward instead of forward. A prime example of this tendency is found in today's passage. When the Israelites did not have the type of food they longed to eat, they considered going back to captivity in order to fill their stomachs with meat.

This consideration offended God. First, the Israelites failed to recognize how God daily provided for their needs. It was a miracle that manna fell from heaven. Second, the Israelites desired to have what they wanted instead of what they needed. Living life based on this formula had the potential to lead them back to a life of slavery instead of forward to a life of freedom.

The Israelites where not the only people who had a wrong perspective of God in this account. Moses did too! When God told Moses He would provide meat for the people, Moses responded to the Lord by saying, "Here I am among six hundred thousand men on foot, and you say, 'I will give them meat to eat for a whole month!' Would they have enough if flocks and herds were slaughtered for them? Would they have enough if all the fish in the sea were caught for them?" (Numbers 11:21–22) Moses definitely had a limited view of God and His ability to provide.

I am not saying that I would not have had the same response as Moses. I probably would have said the same thing. But throughout the Israelites' journey, one theological truth was demonstrated time and time again: God is the plentiful Provider.

In today's verse, God stated His ability to provide for His children in the form of a question: "Is the Lord's arm too short?" Or, to paraphrase, "Is my ability to provide less than your level of need?" The clear answer from scripture is "No!" Numbers 11:31 confirms this truth. "Now a wind went out from the Lord and drove quail in from the sea. It brought them down all around the camp to about three feet above the ground, as far as a day's walk in any direction." Certainly the Lord demonstrated His ability to provide meat for His children and taught the truth that His ability to provide always surpasses any and every need in the believer's life. This is true because God is the plentiful Provider.

We are free to thrive when we recognize that God is our plentiful Provider. As a result, we rest in the Lord's ability to provide for our daily needs. Beware of the tendency to grumble about a lack of provision; you may then fail to recognize how God daily meets your needs. Today, if you feel like you are eating manna in your daily life, thank Him for it. If you long for meat, ask God for meat. Then wait for God's provision to occur in His time and His ways, knowing that He can and will provide for you!

Think About It

Do you need to be reminded that God is your plentiful Provider? If so, please explain your current situation. _____

_____

_____

_____

_____

Have you fallen into the trap of grumbling about your "manna" instead of thanking God for it? _____

_____

_____

_____

_____

Respond To It

Do you have a need in your life? If so, take this opportunity to ask your plentiful Provider to provide for your need. Remember, His ability to provide surpasses any and every need in your life. _____

_____

_____

_____

_____

_____

Day 20:
A Passionate Protector

> *"The Lord will fulfill his purposes for me; your love, O Lord,*
> *endures forever —do not abandon the works of your hand."*
>
> *Psalm 138:8*

Read It

Psalm 138:8 has become a battle cry in my life. "The Lord will fulfill His purposes for me. He will do it!" Two foundational truths are wrapped up in this verse. First, God has a plan for my life. Second, in God's mind, the plan is a done deal. We are free to thrive when we embrace these foundational truths. Dear friend, we do not have to make things happen in our lives. Instead, we can surrender to God's plan and invite Him to work in us and through us for His glory. Through surrendering to God's plan, we can know His will for our lives and hang on to the truth that God's will protects us.

As believers in Jesus Christ, we often fall into two traps when it comes to knowing and doing the will of God. The first trap is the 50/50 partnership trap. This trap occurs each time we view our relationship with God as a partnership where God does 50% of the work while you do the other 50%. This thinking leads to a works-based religion that leaves us asking the question, "Did I do my part?" It compromises spiritual freedom because it places our relationship with God on a scale that measures our ability to accomplish work that only He can do in us and through us.

The second trap is the obedience/blessing trap. Each time we choose obedience solely to secure God's blessing in our lives, we fall into this subtle trap. Even though obedience is good, the root of this trap is a selfish desire to receive blessings from God. In the end, this trap leads to a walk with the Lord that is void of genuine love, devotion, and surrender. Rather, our walk with the Lord becomes defined by what He is or is not doing in our lives.

These wrong perspectives limit freedom by creating a works-based religion that results in bondage. We cannot think that the God of the universe depends on us to get His work accomplished or is somehow forced to work in our lives as a result of our "good" actions. We can know that freedom will not result from believing either of these lies, so we must understand some great, freeing truths!

First, God is not dependent on us or anyone else. Praise His name! God is completely independent and self-sufficient. He is not sitting on His holy throne wondering what will happen next or what He will do if we do not accomplish His work on this earth. Second, God's will for our lives is already established in His perfect, holy mind. Dear friend, God is sovereign. God is outside of time. He already knows every detail of our lives—when we will wake, when we will sleep, and when we will die. He knows everything! How foolish of us to think that we can force God to work in a specific way simply by making the "good" choices in life.

You may be wondering how God's independence and sovereignty relate to Him as our Protector. We can rest in the fact that God and God alone can and will accomplish His work on this earth. Amazingly, God invites sinful humans, who are redeemed by the blood of Jesus Christ, to take part in His work. We take part in the work of the Lord by recognizing that He has a plan for our lives and surrendering to that plan every single day. When we recognize that God has and is in control of that plan, we understand that we do not have to make things happen in our walk with Him. Rather, we are called to daily surrender to His desires for our lives. Thus we tap into the powerful truth that God's will or plan for our lives protects us.

Think about this: God has been protecting your life since the moment you were conceived. In Psalm 139:13 and 16 David states, "For you created my inmost being; you knit me together in my mother's womb...All the days ordained for me were written in your book before one of them came to be." Do you hear David's proclamation? Before you were born, God's will for your life was accomplished. Your days were ordained and written before one of them came to be.

The second way God protects our lives is visible in the finished work of Jesus Christ on the cross. Because of Jesus' death, burial, and resurrection, we have freedom and a God-given ability to live the life God has called us to live—a life of complete surrender and genuine love to our Savior. This is true because the cross provides an opportunity for us to know God in a real, personal way. No longer do we have to wonder if God loves us; He proved it when Jesus died. No longer do you have to ask, "Do you have a plan for my life?" He made provision for that plan in the finished work of Jesus Christ on the cross. In return, we have no need to try to obligate God to work in our lives by making "good" choices. He has already done an amazing work on the cross, and in response we can fall at His feet and genuinely worship Him with all our heart, soul, mind, and strength—the very thing Jesus calls us to do!

Each day you have the chance to take the provision of the cross and allow it to change your life. Know that God has a daily plan for you! The Lord will fulfill His purpose for you. He will do it! Dear sister, you serve the passionate Protector who has been protecting your life since before you were born. Today, surrender to His protection by surrendering to His plan for your life.

Think About It

Have you fallen into the trap of thinking that God is dependent on you to accomplish His work? If so, explain how that has compromised freedom in your life. _____

_____

_____

_____

_____

_____

Do you struggle with the concept that God has a plan for your life and that in God's mind the plan is a done deal? If so, please explain. _____

_____

_____

_____

_____

_____

Respond To It

Each day you are called to surrender to God's holy plan. Without a doubt, you can miss out on God's best if you try and prove yourself to God or live life for yourself. Please journal a prayer expressing your desire to live life protected by God's holy plan, knowing that He will accomplish His plan for your life. He will do it! _____

_____

_____

_____

_____

_____

_____

_____

_____

Week 5:
A God-sized Resolve

"We are free to thrive when we fight a constant fight."

Day 21:
A God-sized Resolve

"Put on the full armor of God, so that when the day of evil comes, you may be able to stand your ground, and after you have done everything, to stand. Stand firm...."

Ephesians 6:13–14

Read It

Have you ever watched two teams battle in a game of tug of war? One side makes progress; then the other side pulls ahead. In the end, the stronger team wins. We can think of our spiritual walks much like a game of tug of war. There are times when we are strong and times when we are weak. Times when we clearly make progress and times when defeat seems one "tug" away. One goal of the Christian walk is spiritual progress: becoming more like Jesus in the way we think, act, and feel, and less like the world in the way we respond to life. We move toward the goal of becoming more like Jesus as we focus on Him and follow His ways, not our own.

In our pursuit of Christ, we will encounter obstacles. One obstacle is our flesh or sinful nature; it's the part of us that longs to do what feels good or temporarily satisfies our desires. Another obstacle is the devil, who does whatever he can do to get us to take our eyes off of Jesus and place them on ourselves. Without a doubt, the devil and our flesh often keep us feeling like we are one tug away from defeat. However, the opposite is true. Because of Jesus' death, burial, and resurrection, the devil and our flesh have been defeated. We have the God-given ability, based on the finished work of Christ on the cross, to overcome the obstacles in our lives!

Both our flesh and the devil work to inhibit our spiritual freedom; we must actively respond to both. The Bible tells us how to respond by instructing us to stand—and not only stand, but to stand firm! Think back to the picture of the tug of war game that was just in your mind. Can you envision a person hanging on to the rope with their heels dug in to the ground, pulling with all their might, and not willing to give up one inch? I hope so. This image represents the daily resolve that we must have in order to fight our flesh and the devil.

Freedom requires a constant fight! To win this fight we must resolve to daily win our tug of war battles, in Jesus' name. We must willingly dig in our heels against our sinful flesh and the schemes of the devil and stand our spiritual ground. Once we have taken a stand, we must take it again, and again, and again, and again.

Each day you must wake up ready to fight. Know that freedom over sin is rightfully yours in Jesus Christ. As you fight, you will experience spiritual progress that allows you to live in the freedom Christ provides. You will have victory in Jesus' name! Before you know it, you will find yourself gaining spiritual ground as your flesh and the devil slowly lose grip on the rope of your life. The war will continue as long as you walk on this earth but you will make progress! So today, make the choice to take hold of the spiritual rope in your life, dig in your heels, and fight, fight, fight!

Think About It

Where are you in the game of spiritual tug of war? Are you living in victory or defeat?

_____

_____

_____

Rate your current level of determination to fight. Circle your answer.

| 1 | 2 | 3 | 4 | 5 | 6 | 7 | 8 | 9 | 10 |

No fighting   Little fighting   Half fighting   Regular fighting   Always fighting

List the spiritual exercises or disciplines that help you fight. _____

_____

_____

_____

Are you ready to fight? If so, describe your level of resolve. _____

_____

_____

_____

Respond To It

Journal a prayer asking the Lord to help you take a spiritual stand by digging in your heels and getting ready to fight. Make a resolve to no longer give up one inch of spiritual ground! Fight, fight, fight!_____

_____

_____

_____

_____

_____

_____

Day 22:
A Good Goal

"Do not be overcome by evil, but overcome evil with good."

Romans 12:21

Read It

The instruction found in Romans 12:21 should provide comfort and reassurance to us as believers in Jesus Christ. Evil can be overcome by good! Hope should flow into our hearts each time we realize this truth. Jesus Christ has secured our victory over sin and death. As a result, the evil in our lives can be defeated!

If we want to walk daily in freedom, we must be battle ready. We are battle ready when we know that we are in a war and we are ready to fight that war. This involves three things:

- Knowing our enemy.
- Knowing his tactics.
- Knowing how to win.

In yesterday's devotion, we identified two primary enemies—our flesh and the devil. Yesterday's devotion explained their tactics. The flesh longs to do the things that make us feel good or temporarily satisfies our desires. The devil does whatever he can to get our eyes off of Jesus so we will place our eyes on ourselves. Knowing these tactics help us to recognize the great need to fight to win in our daily lives. Knowing how to fight to win is crucial. Each devotion this week will focus on how we can win the daily spiritual tug of war battle.

In order to win the spiritual tug of war battle, we need to identify areas of life that are potential pitfalls created by our flesh and the devil. A pitfall is an area where we are likely to sin—one where we are likely to give up spiritual ground by seeking our desires instead of God's desires. Because these pitfalls surround us every single day, we must know them intimately. When we start to slip, we will recognize what is taking place and begin to fight. Pitfalls present themselves in different forms—unhealthy relationships, sinful habits, or wrong heart attitudes.

Once we have identified our possible pitfalls, we are ready for the second step—setting boundaries in these areas to ensure spiritual success. In this context, boundaries are safety measures designed to help us win the spiritual battles we face. Two important components of proper spiritual boundaries are God's Word and accountability partners.

God's Word is essential because it contains God's instructions for how we should live. God's Word is our light in a very dark world; it contains God's wisdom and desires when it comes to dealing with the pitfalls. Many of our pitfalls are identified in the Word of God; the Bible also provides instruction about the best way to deal with them. If we tend to be fearful, the Bible tells us how to have peace by trusting in the Lord.

Taking our pitfalls to the Lord and examining them in light of His Word allows us to be well equipped to respond to our difficulties. If we want to have any chance of winning our spiritual tug of war battles, God's Word must play an active role in our lives. Accountability partners are also critical because we need someone holding us accountable to obey the Word of God. Accountability partners ask the tough questions and tell us what we need to hear, no matter what!

We are free to thrive when we consistently short-circuit the desires of our flesh and the schemes of the devil by knowing the pitfalls in our lives and responding to those areas in a God-honoring way. Without a doubt, God's Word and an accountability partner will help strengthen you to win the spiritual tug of war battles in your life.

Think About It

List the current pitfalls that you face. Please be as specific as possible.

- _____
- _____
- _____
- _____

What does God's Word say about each pitfall? _____
_____
_____

Do you have an accountability partner? Yes   No

If yes, please explain how your accountability partner will help you fight the pitfalls listed above. If no, please list the person you plan to ask to serve as your accountability partner and how that person will help you fight._____
_____
_____
_____

Respond To It

Journal a prayer asking the Lord to help you to fight to win._____
_____
_____
_____
_____
_____

Day 23:
A Clear Focus

"I want to know Christ and the power of his resurrection and the fellowship of his sufferings, becoming like him in his death."

Philippians 3:10

Read It

On an overseas mission trip, I enjoyed a trip to the local market. My task was clear—to find the perfect memento and bring it home. I saw two items that caught my attention. One was a beautiful ring that was unique and just my style; the other was a carved checker set that would provide hours of family fun. Each item was expensive, so I knew I had to make a choice. I could buy the ring for myself or I could buy the checker set for my family. Only one item would return to America. I made the decision based on what I really wanted. I will not admit if I chose the selfish or unselfish purchase, but I will say the ring looks great with many of my outfits!

Daily we make choices based on our desires. If we really want something, we go to great lengths to get it. In the book of Philippians, Paul shared his greatest desire—"I want to know Christ." Plain and simple, Paul wanted to know everything he could know about Jesus Christ. Paul's desire to know Jesus impacted the way he lived his life and brought him to a point where he willing fought for the freedom that was rightfully his in Christ. This willingness to fight represents a key "how to" for winning the spiritual tug of war battles in our lives. We have to want to win!

Paul noted three areas in Philippians 3:10 that fueled his desire to know Jesus. The areas included power, fellowship, and Christ-likeness.

- **Power.** The power described in Philippians 3:10 is not average power. It is the same power that God used to raise Jesus from the dead. The Greek word for power used in this verse is the same root that gives us the English word dynamite. Every believer in Jesus Christ has explosive power living inside of her! This is the kind of power that brings buildings down and moves mountains in a matter of seconds. When we think about our ability to fight our flesh and the devil, we can know that Jesus Christ's dynamite power resides in us, enabling us to fight to win!

- **Fellowship.** The fellowship described in Philippians 3:10 is not the kind of fellowship we experience when we mingle in a crowded room of acquaintances. It's the type of fellowship we have with a person who makes a dramatic difference in our life. Think about the difference between mingling in a crowded room with acquaintances and sitting in your living room talking to your closest friend. Obviously, the fellowship of a close friend is much more meaningful. When we make knowing Jesus our number one passion, we fellowship with Him every moment of the day as we walk closely with Him. The more we know Him, the more we want to know Him. Before long we find that close fellowship with Jesus means that we begin to live a life that imitates Christ. Thus, we will walk in freedom and make the choice to avoid potential pitfalls in our lives.

- **Christ-likeness.** As Paul experienced God's power in his life and recognized the fellowship that came from knowing Him more, Paul naturally became more and more like Christ. By no means was this an easy road for Paul to walk; it cost Paul a great deal. Paul had to learn to abandon his way of life and embrace Christ's way of life. Because Paul desired to know Christ more than he desired to please himself, he became more like Christ in his character and actions. As we make knowing Christ our number one passion, our lives will be freed from the power of sin. It will happen! We will become more like Christ, and Christ is free of sin. Certainly we will never be without sin while living on this earth, but we will make significant spiritual progress.

For a moment, I want you to stop and think about Philippians 3:10. Think about the depth of meaning in these inspired words of Paul. In light of these words, may I ask you one question? What do you really want in your life? I hope you can answer, "I want to know Christ." If so, you can know freedom is at work in you. You can know that you are living a life full of God's **power**, a life experiencing a unique kind of **fellowship**, and a life that allows you to become more and **more like Christ**. In the end, you can know that you are living a free life that allows you to thrive every single day!

Think About It

What is the number one "want" in your life? Please be very honest. _____

_____

_____

_____

_____

How can wanting to know Christ more than anything or anyone position you to fight a constant fight in your daily life? _____

_____

_____

_____

Can you honestly say that you want to win the spiritual battles going on in your life to the point that you are willing to do whatever God calls you to do? Yes   No

If you answered yes, please move to the next section. If you answered no, let me encourage you to stop and seek the Lord. Ask Him to help you want to know Him more than you want anything or anyone in your life. Dear sister, you can know that this is His desire for your life and your path to freedom.

Respond To It

Are you willing to abandon your ways and embrace Christ's? If so, journal a prayer below and state your desire to want Him more every single day. _____

_____

_____

_____

_____

_____

_____

Day 24:
An Abiding Heart

> *"I am the vine; you are the branches. If a man remains in me and I in him, he will bear much fruit; apart from me you can do nothing."*
>
> *John 15:5*

Read It

Fighting a consistent fight requires an abiding heart that understands that we must surrender to God's work to make spiritual progress. In John 15:5, Jesus puts it this way: "I am the vine; you are the branches."

Understanding Jesus' role as the vine requires us to come to the point each day of finding our source of strength in Him. Apart from Christ, there is nothing that we can do on our own, and there is no good thing in us that allows us to win our spiritual battles. Because we are the branches, our job is to respond to the vine. Any spiritual progress that is made in our lives occurs as a direct result of abiding in Jesus the Vine. Each day our focus must be on remaining connected to Jesus Christ. As we do this, our resolve to fight the spiritual battles in our lives will remain strong.

Abiding presents a challenge during easy as well as difficult seasons of life. In easy seasons, our natural tendency is to let our guard down and coast through life believing that we have a handle on things. This attitude can lead us straight into the trap of self-sufficiency, thinking that spiritual battles can be won independently from God. Self-sufficiency means trusting our own abilities to make spiritual progress instead of God's supernatural work in our lives.

Abiding during difficult seasons is equally challenging but in a different way. When seasons are difficult (often during times of intense spiritual battle), our natural human tendency is to run from the work God desires to do in our lives by giving in to the sin or by disengaging and simply ignoring His working.

True abiding occurs when we constantly run to God during the easy as well as difficult times in life. Understanding the call to abide is a key component in winning our spiritual battles. Abiding teaches us to guard our lives from self-sufficiency during the easy times, and it challenges us to stay engaged during the difficult times. In the end, abiding in Jesus is crucial in fighting a constant fight; this abiding positions you to win!

Think About It

Do you find yourself in the midst of an easy or difficult season of life?   Easy   Difficult

If easy, are you falling into the trap of self-sufficiency? If so, please describe. _____

_____

_____

_____

_____

If difficult, are you running from the work God desires to do in your life? If so, please describe. _____

_____

_____

_____

_____

How can you abide in Christ in easy as well as difficult seasons of life? _____

_____

_____

_____

_____

Respond To It

Close with a word of prayer expressing your desire to have an abiding heart—a heart that remains connected to Christ. _____

_____

_____

_____

_____

_____

Day 25:
A Christ-centered Resolve

Jesus said, "The Spirit of the Lord is on me,
because he has anointed me to preach good news
to the poor. He has sent me to proclaim freedom for
the prisoners and recovery of sight for the blind, to release
the oppressed, to proclaim the year of the Lord's favor."

Luke 4:18–19

Read It

As we engage in our constant fights for spiritual freedom, we must have an all-encompassing view of Jesus in our daily lives. This fact cannot be overstated. We must know Jesus and the work He desires to do in us. For just a moment, I want to invite you to consider the way you think about Jesus. Do you think of Jesus as the conquering King? Based on Luke 4:18–19, we can know that Jesus is the conquering King who came to set us free! Wrapped in this truth, we can experience Jesus in His grandness and know Jesus as our Redeemer, Deliverer, and soon-coming King!

Think about Jesus as our Redeemer! Jesus lived a life that only He could live—a life free from sin. Jesus died on the cross and took on Himself the punishment for every wrong thought, action, and motive we ever committed. Jesus paid the price for the sin that separates you and me from God. The result? The moment we call on the name of the Lord, He saves us from our sins and, in God's eyes, moves us from spiritual death to spiritual life. We experience the redeeming work of Jesus in our lives! Knowing Jesus as our Redeemer means that we understand our need for a Savior and that we long for Jesus to change our lives in a very personal way.

Think about Jesus as our Deliverer! Once we are cleansed from our sins and enjoying fellowship with God, sin continues to impact our lives. But we can have hope because we are not helpless in the face of the day-by-day onslaught of sin. The moment Jesus rose from the dead, He proclaimed victory over sin and death and provided us with the necessary power to overcome the grip of sin. Overcoming sin requires a life of complete dependence on Christ, a life that abides in Him. This kind of life longs to be controlled by the Spirit of God as we daily make the choice to fight the sin in our lives based on His power, not our own. This allows us to experience Jesus as our Deliverer!

Think about Jesus as our soon-coming King! Recognizing Jesus as our Redeemer and Deliverer positions us to long for Him to be our soon-coming King. When we are serious about fighting the sin in our lives, we can't help but long for Jesus to return to take us to heaven. We will long to live in a place where we will be free from the sin and death that plague this fallen world. Focusing on Jesus' return allows us to anticipate our real home in heaven with God and provides freedom over the distractions found in this world. Living in anticipation of the day Jesus returns to this earth provides the best way to celebrate Jesus as our soon-coming King. This eternal focus helps us reflect the priorities of Christ as we value the things of eternity over the things of this world.

Recognizing that Jesus is our Redeemer, Deliverer, and soon-coming King helps us fight a constant fight. Going forward, how will you view Jesus in your daily life? Will you see Him as the meek Savior who came as a baby or the conquering King who came to set you free? The beauty of this question is that Jesus is uniquely both! He came in the flesh as a baby to deliver you from your flesh, and He rules as King to provide a way for you to live a complete life in Him!

Think About It

When you think about Jesus, describe the thoughts that come to your mind.

_____
_____
_____
_____
_____
_____

How would it help you fight a constant fight if you viewed Jesus as your Redeemer, Deliverer, and soon- coming King? Please respond to each.

• Redeemer_____
_____
_____
_____

• Deliverer _____
_____
_____
_____

• Soon-coming King_____
_____
_____
_____

Respond To It

Journal a prayer asking the Lord to broaden your perspective of Him. _____

_____

_____

_____

_____

_____

_____

_____

_____

Week 6:
A Willing Spirit

*"We are free to thrive when we
do whatever the Lord asks us to do."*

Day 26:
A Willing Spirit

"Go, sell everything you have and give to the poor, and you will have treasure in heaven. Then come, follow me."

Mark 10:21

Read It

These words must have cut to the heart of the rich young ruler. I believe scripture indicates that the rich man displayed an interest in knowing how to follow Jesus. Mark 10:17–23 presents the full story:

> "As Jesus started on his way, a man ran up to him and fell on his knees before him. 'Good teacher,' he asked, 'what must I do to inherit eternal life?'
>
> 'Why do you call me good?' Jesus answered. 'No one is good—except God alone. You know the commandments: "Do not murder, do not commit adultery, do not steal, do not give false testimony, do not defraud, honor your father and mother."'
>
> 'Teacher,' he declared, 'all these I have kept since I was a boy.'
>
> Jesus looked at him and loved him. 'One thing you lack,' he said. 'Go, sell everything you have and give to the poor, and you will have treasure in heaven. Then come, follow me.' At this the man's face fell. He went away sad, because he had great wealth." (Other accounts of this incident can be found in Matthew 19:16–30 and Luke 18:18–29).

I imagine Jesus' response took the rich man by surprise. Certainly the rich man was not a renegade. He was not out to break any laws. In fact, I believe at some level the rich man wanted to follow Jesus. I base this belief on the action the rich man took as he ran to Jesus and fell at his feet. It was not until the rich man heard the call that Jesus placed on his life to sell everything and give his possessions to the poor that he made the decision to turn away.

Certainly Jesus' instruction to the rich man to sell everything was drastic. Imagine if Jesus asked you to give up ALL your worldly possessions. This means no house, no car, absolutely nothing. How would you respond? I know for me, I would stop and think about the cost of following Jesus. I believe that is exactly what Jesus wanted the rich man to consider—the cost of following Him.

In asking the rich man to give up everything, I believe Jesus issued a call for every follower of Christ—the call to possess a willing spirit. A willing spirit is one that wants Jesus more than anything or anyone else. Without a doubt, the rich man lacked a willing spirit. He lacked a willingness to give up control of at least one area of his life—his resources. The rich man longed to hang on to his finances more than he wanted to follow Jesus. To the rich man, his resources may have represented security, prominence, and self-sufficiency, the very things the world told the rich man to achieve.

Jesus longed for the rich man to have a spirit that freely gave to Jesus no matter the cost. Unfortunately, the rich man did not possess this kind of spirit. As a result, the rich man walked away from Jesus and straight into the arms of captivity as he made the choice to serve his riches rather than his Creator.

Today we have the same choice. Will we serve the things of this world or will we serve the Creator of this world? If we choose to value any area of our lives more than we value God, we allow bondage to take the place of freedom as we fail to display a willing spirit. We are free to thrive when we want Jesus more than we want anything else; as a result, we are willing to give everything to Jesus in order to follow His plans, not our own. Embracing a willing spirit goes against everything the world promotes. The world says, "Hang on to everything." Jesus invites, "Value Me more than anything." What will you choose?

Think About It

What area(s) of life do you value more than Jesus? Please list each area here.

_____

_____

_____

_____

_____

Do you believe Jesus is calling you to give these areas to Him?   Yes   No

How will giving these areas to Jesus set you free to thrive?_____

_____

_____

_____

_____

_____

Respond To It

Please journal a prayer asking the Lord to help you display a willing spirit—a spirit that wants Him more than you want anything else! _____

_____

_____

_____

_____

_____

_____

Day 27:
A Righteous Faith

"The righteous will live by faith."

Romans 1:17

Read It

These six simple words really are not simple at all. Living by faith and not by sight represents one of the great struggles in the Christian life. Unfortunately, we live in a day and age where faith seems obsolete, even within the church. Our culture says, "You have to prove something, or I will never believe it." Today's generation embraces an "I have to see it to believe it" type of approach to life where even believers place more faith in the seen things of the world than the unseen things of God. The result is that we are a "smart" and "refined" generation that often forsakes righteous faith in God alone.

I wonder if this is true in your life. How many times have you thought or said, "Lord, I need you to prove your love to me by doing this"? To me, this indicates a practice of living by sight where we have to see something, touch it, or manipulate it in order to believe it. This attitude creates a never-ending cycle that constantly places God on trial to prove His love and devotion to us.

The heart of the Father must be grieved when believers take this approach to the Christian life. Any time we forsake faith in Christ's daily provision, we compromise our freedom in Christ. If we say, "Lord, you have to prove yourself to me," we display an unwillingness to recognize who He is and what He has already done. We have lost the ability to radically believe Him, no matter what. We have compromised our faith and we no longer stake our claim on His great ability to work no matter how overwhelming our circumstances appear to be.

I remember the day when the Lord confronted my tendency to live by sight. I was walking at a local walking track. As I walked, I prayed. I asked the Lord to prove His love to me by doing something very specific on my behalf. Immediately, the Lord brought to my mind Romans 5:8. "But God demonstrates his own love for us in this: While we were still sinners Christ died for us." This verse brought a sense of freedom into my life. I realized that God did not need to prove anything to me. He had already proven everything to me when He sent Jesus to die in my place.

Today, you face a choice. Will you place your trust in the Lord as you embrace a life lived by faith not by sight? If so, begin to dream. You are about to enter the most amazing adventure in life. No longer will you feel the need to ask God to prove Himself to you. A new sense of freedom will come into your life as you understand that God has already proven His love. Now you have the opportunity to respond to God's love every single day as you live by faith. The very reality of your life will become, "Lord, whatever you say, I will do. Lord, wherever you send me, I will go." Yes, we will be free to thrive when we embrace a life lived by faith!

Think About It

When was the last time you lived by faith and not by sight? Please explain here.

_____

_____

_____

_____

_____

How often do you find yourself asking God to prove His love to you? How does this action compromise your freedom in Christ? _____

_____

_____

_____

_____

_____

Respond To It

Please journal a prayer asking the Lord to help you embrace a life lived by faith, not by sight. _____

_____

_____

_____

_____

_____

_____

_____

_____

Day 28:
A Limit-free Life

*"Now the Lord is the Spirit, and where the
Spirit of the Lord is, there is freedom."*

2 Corinthians 3:17

Read It

I love boxes, cubbies, containers, and organizers—anything that has compartments! Why? Compartments make me feel like I am in control as I think, "This goes here, and that goes there." Unfortunately, things are not the only items I have tried to contain. At times, I have also treated God this way when I said, "Lord, you can go here, but you are not invited to go there." Naturally, God did not subscribe to my way of thinking and graciously took the necessary steps in order to straighten me out!

A limit-free life recognizes that we are free to thrive when all barriers or compartments in our relationship with Christ are removed. Paul stated it this way in 2 Corinthians 3:17: "Where the Spirit of the Lord is, there is freedom." This represents an amazing paradox found in scripture. Freedom is not controlling our own lives. Rather, we are free to thrive when we are controlled by Christ! The world we live in (as well as our sinful flesh) often balks at this truth. However, scripture makes it clear—we are free when we live compartment-free, Christ-controlled lives!

Achieving a limit-free life requires diligence in God's Word. It is a life that is disciplined to seek God through His Word every day. Using the teachings found in the Bible we can establish God's authority over our lives by remembering that God is God and we are not. Certainly God does not need this reminder, but we do. As we establish God's authority over our lives, we will see that all compartments are removed as we recognize Jesus as leader of every area of our lives. The following routine provides a tangible way for you to live a limit-free life in Jesus Christ.

I establish God's authority over every area of my life when I remember who God is and who I am in relationship to God. Each morning I wake up and affirm:

- "God, today You are my Creator, and I am your creation."
- "Jesus, today You are my Vine, and I am your branch."
- "Jesus, today You are my Shepherd, and I am your sheep."
- "Holy Spirit, today You are my Teacher, and I am your student."
- "God, today You are my Father, and I am your child."
- "Jesus, today You are my Savior, and I am a sinner."
- "God, today You are my Potter, and I am the clay."

As I wake up and proclaim these truths, I am reminded that I need God in every single area of my life. I cannot make it on my own, and I must fight the tendency to compartmentalize my life. I am free to thrive as I invite the Spirit of the Lord to reign supreme in every area that I tend to keep "off limits" to Him.

Today, when you find yourself compartmentalizing areas of your life, make the choice to surrender every area of your life to the Lord. Invite Jesus to show you His kind of freedom—the freedom that comes as He controls your life.

Think About It

Is there an area or two in your life that you tend to keep "off limits" to God? If so, please describe that area. _____

_____

_____

_____

How has keeping this area "off limits" affected your level of freedom?_____

_____

_____

_____

How can daily establishing God's authority over your life help you surrender your "off limits" areas?_____

_____

_____

_____

_____

Respond To It

Today, I want to challenge you to embrace a limit-free life by removing the compartments and turning to the Lord. Use the space below to state your desire and ask for the Lord's help. _____

_____

_____

_____

_____

_____

_____

_____

Day 29:
A Powerful Information Supply

"This is what the LORD says, he who made the earth,
the LORD who formed it and established it, the LORD
is his name: 'Call to me and I will answer you and tell
you great and unsearchable things you do not know.'"

Jeremiah 33:2–3

Read It

The invitation is clear. God says, "Call on me." The result? "I will answer you." What does God promise to provide? Great things—things we cannot know apart from Him. Wow! God certainly offers a powerful information supply when it comes to living our daily lives! Our choice is seen in our willingness to accept His information into our lives.

We are free to thrive when we look to God for answers. Once we realize that God has the answer because He is the answer, we are able to stop trying to define our own problems and striving to solve them. We begin to see each day as an opportunity to call on God and listen for His sweet reply. Our response to His reply produces in us a willing spirit that does whatever the Lord asks us to do.

In Jeremiah 33:2, the prophet Jeremiah pointed to a key character quality or attribute found in God that allows Him to make promises and supply answers for our daily lives—His ability to create things from nothing. God is the Creator God. The ability to create is held by God alone. There is no other being that can say, "Look, I created that. I started with nothing, and now there is something." Sure, all humans can make things. We can take some of this and some of that and mix it together to produce a new product. However, no one but God can begin with nothing and finish with something.

You are free to thrive when you recognize that God alone creates. He made you. He knows you. He willingly provides for you. Your response must be to listen to Him and respond to His call. Embracing the truth that God knows things that are unknown to you must be a daily resolve. You can then position your heart to hear from God, making Him your powerful information supply. "Call on me," God says. When you do, you can know that God will share great things with you—things you cannot know apart from Him. Today, have you called on Him? If not, stop right now and turn to your Creator God. Pour out your heart to Him, and then prepare yourself for His reply. Submit right now to whatever your Creator is calling you to do.

Think About It

Have you thought about how God's ability to create things, including you, gives Him the ability to provide a powerful information supply in your daily life? Yes No

Please explain how this process works. _____

_____

_____

_____

_____

Compare and contrast a believer and a non-believer when it comes to each person's available information supply.

• Believer: _____

_____

_____

_____

_____

• Non-believer: _____

_____

_____

_____

_____

Respond To It

Journal a prayer asking the Lord to help you see Him as Creator God. Ask Him to help you know that because He created you, you should turn to Him for direction in your life._____

_____

_____

_____

_____

_____

_____

_____

Day 30:
A Willingness to Learn

*"Teach me to do your will, for you are my God; may your
good Spirit lead me on level ground." Psalm 143:10*

Read It

Recently I went on an overnight backpacking adventure with a good friend who is an avid backpacker. She owns all the equipment and thrives in outdoor scenarios; I, on the other hand, thrive in hotels. I am not, however, the type of person who backs down from a challenge; for twenty-four hours I was a backpacker. Of course, I knew nothing about backpacking when I started the process, so I had to learn by watching my friend. I had to listen to her important instructions and follow them. Once we were on the hike, I had to imitate my friend's actions and reactions. I enjoyed my backpacking adventure and learned so much. Who knows, I might even do it again!

In our relationship with Christ, we must be willing to learn. In fact, we are free to thrive when we are willing to learn something new every single day. Psalm 143:10 conveys the reason why believers in Christ must be willing to learn. God is our God, and we need to be led by Him and the Spirit He placed inside our hearts at the moment of salvation.

For just a moment, I want you to think about a time when you were in school. When I was in school, I learned in two different settings. Classroom learning took place every day and often required a specific time, a set place, a designated textbook, and a qualified teacher. It required diligence and commitment to the learning process. The second setting was the laboratory. The lab provided a time for me to take the information that I learned in the classroom and put that information into practice through hands-on experiments. The lab was challenging and exciting because it allowed me to demonstrate my ability to process and implement the material that I had learned.

With these two ideas in mind, let's think about the way we learn from the Lord. I think of the classroom setting as my daily personal quiet time in the Word. In these times, I am sitting before the Lord with my Bible open, and I am asking the Holy Spirit to teach me. My desire is for the Holy Spirit to fill my head and my heart with life-changing truths. I think of the lab setting as my day-in-and-day-out walk with the Lord, my experiences inside and outside my home. During these experiences the Lord teaches me through different encounters with people and circumstances. The lessons may be exciting or painful. They may be expected or take me by surprise. I may respond well to the situation, or I may mess up. No matter the outcome, one thing I can know for sure. My success or failure in the lab is a direct reflection of what I did or did not learn in the classroom.

Psalm 143:10 talks about the Spirit of God leading us on level ground. We walk on level ground as we embrace a willingness to learn in the classroom setting and then a desire to live out that learning in the lab setting. A walk on level ground does not shift with the changing tide of the world or even the ever-changing desires in our hearts. Rather, a walk on level ground is a life that is sensitive to the leading and guiding of the Holy Spirit. In fact, do you want to know the key component of walking on level ground? It is an undeniable and unquenchable thirst for the Spirit of God to lead you and guide you every single moment of your day. In John 14:26 we learn that the role of the Holy Spirit in our lives is to teach us (as seen in the classroom setting) and remind us (as seen in the lab setting.) Today, embrace your need for the leading and guiding of the Holy Spirit by demonstrating a willingness to learn. As you do, know that you are free to thrive every step of the way!

Think About It

Describe a time when you had to look to someone else in order to learn a skill or a lesson in your life._____

_____

_____

_____

_____

_____

Where do you learn best? In the classroom or in the lab? _____

_____

_____

_____

_____

_____

What is God teaching you right now? If you embrace this teaching, how will it lead to freedom in your life?_____

_____

_____

_____

_____

_____

_____

_____

Respond To It

Journal a prayer asking the Lord to teach you with His good Spirit. Ask Him to lead you on level ground. _____

_____

_____

_____

_____

_____

_____

_____

_____

_____

_____

_____

Week 7:
A Desperate Dependence on Christ

*"We are free to thrive when we
pass the point of no return."*

Day 31:
A Desperate Dependence on Christ

"'You do not want to leave too, do you?' Jesus asked the Twelve. Simon Peter answered him, 'Lord, to whom shall we go? You have the words of eternal life. We believe and know that you are the Holy One of God.'"

John 6:67–69

Read It

Jesus asked His disciples an important question at a pivotal point in His earthly ministry. "You do not want to leave too, do you?" Jesus' teachings were transitioning from focusing primarily on outward signs of awe and wonder as seen in the miracles that He performed to a time when Jesus called for inward change of the heart by challenging His followers to know Him as their Savior. Scripture indicates that the response to this time of transition was telling. Many "followers" left the Lord's movement. As they left, the Lord turned to the Twelve and asked, "You do not want to leave too, do you?" Simon replied, "Lord, to whom shall we go?"

The response of Simon and the other disciples provides a picture of desperate dependence on Jesus Christ. The disciples' desperation evidenced itself in a willingness to place all of their hope in Jesus. No longer would the disciples straddle the fence, make a list of other options, or wait to see how things turned out. They had passed the point of no return—the point where their hearts were closer to Jesus and heaven than to man and this world.

We are free to thrive when we pass the point of no return—when our hearts are closer to Jesus and heaven than to people and this world. Reaching this point requires ardent faith. It requires us to embrace a life lived outside of our comfort zones and beyond our resource supply, when our reality becomes, "Lord, if you do not get me through, I will not make it!"

The key to living this kind of life is found in the truth Peter spoke when he recognized Jesus as the Holy One of God. He is the only One who can make sense of our lives and provide hope. Jesus provides peace. He is all we need to make it through each day. Knowing and believing these truths strengthens our faith and protects us from responding like the "followers" who ran when the Lord's teachings transitioned from outward signs of awe and wonder to an inward call of belief.

Daily we are called to make a choice. Will we run, or will we remain? Running demonstrates a life that follows Jesus when things are easy and it seems He is working for us. Remaining demonstrates a desperate dependence on Christ no matter how tough things get. As we remain, we will be asked one question, "You do not want to leave too, do you?" Dear friend, your reply to this question determines if you are walking in the freedom Christ provides. We are free to thrive when we consistently reply, "Lord, to whom shall we go?"

Think About It

When things get tough, do you run like the "followers" who left the Lord's movement or do you remain like Peter and his friends? _____

_____

_____

Describe a time when you ran from the Lord because times were tough._____

_____

_____

_____

_____

Looking back, did running compromise your freedom in Christ? If so, please explain.

_____

_____

_____

_____

Describe a time when you remained when things were tough. What did this experience teach you about freedom?_____

_____

_____

_____

_____

Respond To It

Journal a prayer and ask the Lord to help pass the point of no return in your daily walk with Him. _____

_____

_____

_____

_____

Day 32:
A Source for Competence

"Not that we are competent in ourselves to claim anything for ourselves, but our competence comes from God."

2 Corinthians 3:5

Read It

As you read today's verse, can I hear an "Amen"? This verse comes alive for me every time I stand in front of a group to speak or sit in front of my computer to write. God provides the competence I need to do the work He calls me to do. I am free to thrive as I embrace this truth and live out of His competence, not my own.

Allow me to share a few details about my life. When I was a child, I struggled with dyslexia and had trouble reading and writing. For the first six years of grade school, I spent time in remedial classes. Very few summers went by that I didn't attend some kind of summer school or receive some kind of special instruction. As a result, my level of confidence to do anything like reading, writing, or speaking was extremely low.

As God began to stir a desire in my heart to teach women His word and to write Bible studies, I did not think those things would be possible. I didn't feel confident reading in public, and the mechanics of grammar, punctuation, and spelling challenged me. As I struggled with my desire to teach and write, I spent many nights tossing and turning thinking, "Lord, I cannot do this!"

Freedom came as I embraced the truth that I did not have to possess all the necessary resources to accomplish God's work in my life. Instead, the resources would be provided as I daily followed God's plan, willingly listening to Him and obeying. Over the years, God brought people into my life that helped me. These people served as my mentors and pointed out abilities in my life that I could not see. They helped me hone the skills that I did not know I had. Through it all, God became my Teacher, and I slowly realized that He was going to allow me to do things I never dreamed possible. However, I would have to rely on God and daily trust Him to do the speaking and writing work in me and through me.

Today freedom comes in the same way. We must learn to rely on God. We must surrender to the truth that we do not have to have all the necessary resources to accomplish God's will in our lives. In fact, if we think we do, we are most likely not in God's will. Why? Because God desires to take us to a place of desperate dependence, a place where it is clearly God at work in us—a place where our abilities mean nothing and His abilities mean everything. In short, this is a place where we find our source of competence in God's ability to work not our own.

Think About It

Are you living based on God's competence or your own? In other words, are you doing things that you can accomplish in your own strength or are you doing things that only God can accomplish through you? _____

_____

_____

_____

_____

_____

Please describe some aspect of God's plan for your life that is outside your abilities (an area of your life where you must lean on God)._____

_____

_____

_____

_____

_____

How can leaning on God in this area lead to freedom? _____

_____

_____

_____

_____

_____

Respond To It

Journal a prayer asking the Lord to take you to a place where you are living life based on His competence and not your own. _____

_____

_____

_____

_____

_____

_____

Day 33:
A Real Power Source

"Because the hand of the LORD my God
was on me, I took courage and gathered
leading men from Israel to go up with me."

Ezra 7:28

Read It

Ezra is one of my favorite Bible characters. Ezra knew the value of God's Word. As a result, he devoted his life to teaching others God's precepts and decrees. God placed a specific call on Ezra's life. This meant that God placed a very clear task before Ezra and challenged Ezra to accomplish the task. The task God placed before Ezra involved returning from Babylonian captivity to a demolished Jerusalem in order to set up civil order and religious practices. This call placed Ezra in a position of desperate dependence. Ezra did not have the ability to accomplish the task on his own. Ezra had to rely on God.

For just a moment, think about Ezra's difficult position. He was living in captivity in another country because his nation turned its back on God. While in captivity, God called him to take men back to his homeland and rebuild the nation's civil and religious infrastructure. In this call, Ezra was asked to take something that was completely broken and put it back together—piece by piece. Ezra responded, "Because the hand of the Lord my God was on me, I took courage."

I love two things about this verse. First, God's hand was on Ezra. Rebuilding Jerusalem was not Ezra's idea. It was God's idea. As a result, Ezra could respond to God in faith because he knew that God would accomplish this call in his life. Second, as Ezra responded to God in faith, he had the chance to take God's courage into his life. I can't help but imagine a visible picture of Ezra lifting his open palm to the sky, grasping God's life-changing power, and taking hold of it for himself.

Each day we are free to thrive when we do the same. In the face of difficult life circumstances or overwhelming calls, we too must recognize the tasks God is calling us to accomplish. We must know that these tasks will be bigger than anything we can accomplish on our own. God will do the work in us and through us. Finally, we must lift our open palms towards heaven and take hold of God's life-changing power so we can accomplish the tasks in our lives.

For just a moment, think about the source of power you use in your life. We can choose between using God's life-changing power or trying to manufacture our own power. Manufactured power comes from tapping into a power source inside of you like human abilities, resources, or emotions. This power often flows from insecurities, pride, arrogance, and self-will. Although we can accomplish things with this kind of power source, it requires a lot of work and often leads to frustration and exhaustion. The battle cry for the person using manufactured power might be, "I will do it on my own—no matter what!"

In contrast, we must depend on God's life-changing power. This power comes from tapping into a power source outside of us. Like Ezra, we need to realize the best power source in life is God. God's power flows in a never-ending, always-sufficient supply. God's Word provides one avenue by which we can tap into God's power supply. Every promise, every principle, and every precept becomes an avenue for us to know and experience God's power in our daily lives. We are free to thrive when we tap into God's power supply by recognizing that it is God's hand at work in our lives and not our own. When we do this, God's life-changing power flows in and through us as His courage becomes our courage. This courage becomes the power of God at work in our lives. When we use God's power, we can say, "I know that I can't do this on my own—but God can!"

Today, I encourage you to lift your open palm to the sky and grasp God's life-changing power for your life. As you do, know that you are demonstrating a desperate dependence on Christ that connects you to the biggest and best power source available in life. Know that courage will flow in you and through you as you live based on a real power source— God's overwhelming power supply!

Think About It

Based on the definitions provided in this devotion, please explain the difference between manufactured power and God's life-changing power. _____

_____

_____

_____

_____

Which type of power is currently at work in your life? _____

_____

_____

_____

_____

Explain how God's life-changing power leads to freedom as you answer God's call in your life. _____

_____

_____

_____

_____

Respond To It

Journal a prayer asking the Lord to daily help you utilize His life-changing power.

_____

_____

_____

_____

_____

Day 34:
A Transparent Heart

> *"You have no part or share in this ministry, because*
> *your heart is not right before God. Repent of this*
> *wickedness and pray to the Lord. Perhaps he will*
> *forgive you for having such a thought in your heart.*
> *For I see that you are full of bitterness and captive to sin."*
>
> *Acts 8:22–23*

Read It

These strong words flowed from the mouth of Peter to Simon the Sorcerer. Can you imagine the intensity that must have filled the air as Peter called Simon to repentance? What I find interesting about this exchange is the context of the story.

After Stephen was stoned, "a great persecution broke out against the church at Jerusalem, and all except the apostles were scattered throughout Judea and Samaria" (Acts 8:1). Philip, who was a deacon and evangelist, traveled to Samaria where he led many people to faith in Jesus Christ. Scripture gives a moving account of Philip's time in Samaria—especially his encounter with a man named Simon:

"When the crowds heard Philip and saw the miraculous signs he did, they all paid close attention to what he said. With shrieks, evil spirits came out of many, and many paralytics and cripples were healed. So there was great joy in that city. Now for some time a man named Simon had practiced sorcery in the city and amazed all the people of Samaria. He boasted that he was someone great, and all the people, both high and low, gave him their attention and exclaimed, "This man is rightly called the Great Power of God." They followed him because he had amazed them for a long time with his sorcery. But when they believed Philip as he proclaimed the good news of the kingdom of God and the name of Jesus Christ, they were baptized.... Simon himself believed and was baptized." (Acts 8:6–13)

Simon had the ability to make the impossible seem possible. Scripture states that Simon had the attention of everyone in his community. As a result, a few eyebrows must have been raised when this sorcerer appeared to lay down his "magic" power in order to follow Jesus.

Word of Philip's success in Samaria made its way back to Jerusalem. "When the apostles in Jerusalem heard that Samaria had accepted the word of God, they sent Peter and John to them" (Acts 8:14). Once there, Peter and John prayed for the new believers and laid hands on them, and the believers in Samaria received the Holy Spirit.

Simon the Sorcerer took note of their actions and longed to have the same ability in his life. "When Simon saw that the Spirit was given at the laying on of the apostles' hands, he offered them money and said, 'Give me also this ability so that everyone on whom I lay my hands may receive the Holy Spirit" (Acts 8:18–19).

Peter was taken aback by Simon's request. The request put front and center the condition of Simon's heart. His heart was full of bitterness and was captive to sin. Peter stated, "May your money perish with you, because you thought you could buy the gift of God with money!" (Acts 8:20). Peter then called Simon to repentance. Simon responded to Peter's stern warning by asking Peter to pray for him.

Although we do not know if Simon came to a point of true repentance in his heart, we can learn a valuable lesson from this account in scripture. The lesson involves possessing a transparent heart—a heart that is free from sin and displays an understanding that God's favor cannot be bought, earned, or secured apart from Jesus Christ. This was the important lesson that Simon failed to understand. He longed to have the same abilities that Peter and John possessed, but he did not have a heart that was fully committed to Jesus Christ. Simon longed for the power of God, but he missed the important step of living his life in desperate dependence on Christ. Today we can know that any time we take the wrong approach to securing God's power, we fail to possess a transparent heart. A transparent heart has the power of God flowing through it because we live our lives for Him.

Freedom flows through the life of a person who possesses a transparent heart. This type of heart cannot be obtained through good behavior, giving of resources, or following a list of "do's" and "don'ts." A transparent heart is a gift from God through Jesus Christ and comes as we live our lives in desperate dependence on Him.

Allow me to share the application point this devotion brings to my life. I have often struggled with thinking that I can somehow secure God's blessing with my "good" behavior. This mindset has been so strong that at times I found myself grading my personal walk with God based on a list of "do's" and "don'ts." To be honest, there are times when I still fight this tendency. One example involves my speaking ministry. I have to guard against the tendency of trying to earn God's blessing over my speaking events by carefully following a list of standards just prior to an event. In my wrong thinking, I hope that my good behavior will secure God's blessing in my life. This wrong thinking is similar to Simon's wrong thinking. Simon's story teaches me that God's blessing cannot be bought, earned, or secured apart from Jesus Christ. Therefore, when I try to obtain

God's blessing apart from Christ, I am wrong and fail to display a transparent heart. Certainly it is not wrong for me to do the "right" things. However, I must do the right things in the right way and for the right reasons.

Please take a moment and ask the Holy Spirit to examine your heart and show you areas in your life where you have tried to buy, earn, or secure God's favor apart from Christ and thus you have forsaken a transparent heart. If you, like Simon, long to have spiritual fruit that is evident in your life, embrace your desperate need for Jesus Christ. Forsake the tendency of trying to earn God's favor. You can't do it! God's favor is a gift that flows in your life and through your life as you possess a transparent heart before Him.

Think About It

Do you try to earn, buy, or secure God's approval in your life? If so, please explain.

_____

_____

_____

Please define a transparent heart in your own words. _____

_____

_____

_____

How does a desire for a transparent heart bring you to a place of desperate dependence on Jesus Christ? _____

_____

_____

_____

Respond To It

Journal a prayer asking the Lord to grant you a transparent heart before Him.

_____

_____

_____

_____

_____

_____

_____

Day 35:
A God-honoring Timeline

"Little by little I will drive them out before you, until
you have increased enough to take possession of the land."

Exodus 23:30

Read It

Have you ever longed to be at a different place in your life? If so, you know waiting is HARD! Waiting is hard even when we trust the Lord and believe He is at work. We can still wonder, "Lord, will this ever happen?" I imagine the Israelites asked this question as they faced the task of taking and possessing the promised land of Canaan. They knew God was calling them to a certain future even though it seemed out of reach.

In today's verse, God taught the Israelites the importance of a God-honoring timeline. God said, "Little by little I will drive them out." The certainty of this passage grips me. I can almost hear God saying, "My children, this will happen! I will wipe out the Amorites, Hittites, Perizzites, Canaanites, Hivites, and Jebusites. You will dwell in the land I promised to Abraham, Isaac, and Jacob—it will happen!"

God did not drive the foreign nations out of Israel's land quickly. Even though He could have spoken and the land would have been immediately evacuated, God took a different approach. He drove out the foreign nations little by little as a way to teach His children how to grow in their faith. As a result, the Israelites had to wait and watch as God worked on their behalf. This waiting process provided time for God to develop the Israelites into a people who could properly possess the land He willing provided.

Can you relate to the situation the Israelites faced? Perhaps there is a place you long to be—not necessarily a physical place but something you long to do or the type of person you long to be. If so, you are free to thrive when you bring your desire before the Lord and ask Him to reveal His will for your life. Be prepared! God may confirm your desire, or He may redirect your desire. If God confirms it, be patient and submit to the work He is doing in your life even if it seems "little by little." If God redirects, freedom comes as you embrace His new direction for your life.

Often the possession of specific land in our lives occurs as we live "little by little," trusting that God is at work in us, through us, and around us. For just a moment, think how often the areas where you are called to wait and watch become the very avenues God uses to produce Christ-like character in your life. Dear friend, waiting is hard but necessary. You are free to thrive when you accept this truth and know that God uses times of waiting to prepare you to rightly possess the land He freely provides. If you long to be in a different place in your life, thank God that He is at work in you, through you, and around you even though the work may seem to be progressing "little by little." Today you can display a desperate dependence on God as you live your life according to His timeline, not your own.

Think About It

Do you struggle with living your life according to God's timeline, not your own?

_____

_____

_____

_____

_____

List the areas where God is calling you to wait and watch. _____

_____

_____

_____

_____

_____

Explain how waiting and watching in these areas produces spiritual freedom in your life.

_____

_____

_____

_____

_____

Respond To It

Journal a prayer asking the Lord to help you view life from His timeline, not your own.

_____

_____

_____

_____

_____

_____

_____

_____

Week 8:
A Longing for Home

*"We are free to thrive when we
long for our real home."*

Day 36:
A Longing for Home

> *"Pharaoh asked him, 'How old are you?' Jacob said to*
> *Pharaoh, 'The years of my pilgrimage are a hundred and*
> *thirty. My years have been few and difficult, and they*
> *do not equal the years of the pilgrimage of my fathers.'"*
>
> *Genesis 47:8–9*

Read It

Pharaoh's question seemed simple. He asked Jacob, "How old are you?" Jacob's response was not a simple one. He answered, "The years of my pilgrimage are a hundred and thirty."

In this exchange, we see Jacob's heart as he recognized that he was on a journey—a journey to his real home. Although the earthly journey that provided the context for today's passage could have offered Jacob a sense of fulfillment or completion in his life, the text points to the fact that it did not. Jacob continually focused his heart on his real home.

If you will recall, Jacob's beloved son Joseph had disappeared when he was sent by his father to the hill country to check on his brothers. Joseph's brothers, who were jealous of him, sold Joseph into slavery and then returned home to inform their father of Joseph's "death." The brothers even provided bloodstained clothes to support their story. Jacob took the news of Joseph's "death" very hard. Thankfully, Joseph did not die. By God's providence, Joseph ended up in Egypt.

As the years went by, Jacob carried on with his life until the family experienced something so difficult that they had to look for help outside of their homeland. Canaan and the surrounding areas experienced a severe famine, and Jacob sent his sons to Egypt to buy food. When the sons met the man who was in charge of selling food, it was Joseph. Joseph recognized his brothers and, after a number of interesting events, revealed his identity. Joseph sent word to Jacob that he was still alive and that the entire family was invited to move from Canaan to Egypt.

I am sure that in many ways the move from Canaan to Egypt could have provided Jacob with a sense of fulfillment in his life. Jacob was reunited with his beloved son Joseph. The missing years for this father/son duo would not be recovered, but in many ways their relationship had time to be restored. Also, in Egypt, Jacob and his family escaped the harsh realities of the famine because Joseph was in a position to care for them.

Although Jacob must have experienced some relief in his life as a result of his move from Canaan to Egypt, I believe that scripture indicates Jacob remained focused on his real home. I base this belief on the words Jacob expressed to Pharaoh. When asked, "How old are you?" Jacob responded in a telling way. "The years of my pilgrimage are a hundred and thirty." What an interesting response for Jacob to give! Instead of saying, "I am a hundred and thirty years old," Jacob used the concept of a pilgrimage to describe his physical age. Without a doubt, the concept of a pilgrimage conveys the idea of going on a trip that has a very definite point of destination as a result of a belief that you hold near and dear to your heart. I believe that the pilgrimage that Jacob described was a pilgrimage to his real home in heaven. The word for *pilgrimage* used in the original Hebrew text means to live as a stranger in this world. From this definition, I believe that we can conclude that Jacob possessed a daily resolve to live as a stranger in this world by understanding that he was on a journey to his real home in heaven.

The idea of living as a stranger is also found in the New Testament. In 1 Peter, the apostle Peter urged his readers to have the same resolve. 1 Peter 2:11–12 states, "Dear friends, I urge you as aliens and strangers in this world, to abstain from sinful desires, which war against your soul. Live such good lives among the pagans that, though they accuse you of doing wrong, they may see your good deeds and glorify God on the day he visits us." God's Word is amazing. In both the Old and New Testaments, believers are encouraged to live as strangers in this world.

Today do you view your life as a journey to your real home? Can you say with certainty that this world is not your home? If so, you are experiencing freedom as you fix your eyes on your real home in heaven.

Think About It

Do you struggle with the tendency to focus on this world as your real home? _____

_____

_____

_____

_____

If so, how does this focus compromise your freedom in Christ? _____

_____

_____

_____

_____

How can viewing your life as a pilgrimage to your real home in heaven position you to walk in freedom? _____

_____

_____

_____

_____

_____

Today, how can you live as a stranger in this world? _____

_____

_____

_____

_____

_____

Respond To It

Journal a prayer asking the Lord to grant you a longing for your real home. _____

_____

_____

_____

_____

_____

_____

Day 37:
A Blessed Life

> *"Blessed is she who has believed that what*
> *the Lord has said to her will be accomplished!"*
>
> *Luke 1:45*

Read It

The words found in Luke 1:45 were spoken by Elizabeth, mother of John the Baptist, to Mary, mother of Jesus, following Mary's response to the news of Jesus' conception and soon-coming birth.

For just a moment, place yourself in Mary's position. You are a young woman. You are engaged to be married to a man named Joseph. You have your whole life ahead of you when suddenly an angel appears to you and delivers life-altering news: the long-awaited Messiah is coming, and He is coming through you, a virgin! Talk about a lot of information to process in a short amount of time.

If any person on this earth ever had a reason to doubt God's work in her life, it was Mary. Think about it—a virgin birth! In order to give birth, one thing must happen, and virginity excludes that one thing from happening. In light of this fact, I believe that Mary needed to hear the word of encouragement Elizabeth provided. She needed to know that God blessed those who believed in Him. Securing this blessing required Mary to place her complete faith and trust in God. As Mary placed her complete faith and trust in God, the impossible circumstance of a virgin giving birth to a child became possible.

After Mary gave birth to Jesus, she watched Him develop and grow. Mary had a front row seat to Jesus' time on this earth. Perhaps Mary saw Jesus take His first step. Certainly Mary saw Jesus grow into a man who died on the cross to provide freedom for those who will believe. I wonder if Mary ever thought or asked the question, "Is this the blessed life I was suppose to live?" Certainly there were times when Mary did not understand the events in her life. Perhaps Mary did not come to the place of fully understanding the meaning of blessed until she neared the end of her time on this earth. I base this possibility on the meaning of the word blessed used in Luke 1:45.

A blessed life from God's perspective is different than a blessed life from the world's perspective. A blessed life from the world's perspective involves having an easy or comfortable life on this earth. A blessed life from God's perspective occurs when God is active in a person's life to bring glory to Himself. As a result, the blessed person lives in the very presence of God. I believe this is how Mary lived her life—in the very presence of God. I base this belief on the testimony of Mary's life in scripture. From the beginning, Mary was with Jesus. Mary knew Jesus was the Messiah and encouraged Jesus to begin His earthly ministry. Mary saw Jesus willingly die on the cross. Finally, Mary was with the disciples after Jesus ascended into heaven. Although Mary and Jesus were with each other, she still faced hard times. This may have caused Mary to question the meaning of God's blessing in her life.

If we live very long, we will also experience hard times. I believe the beauty of scripture comes to life when we understand that hard times do not exclude the blessing of God. Sometimes the greatest blessings in life come as we walk through the hard times knowing that God is with us and that when we cannot walk, He willingly carries us.

How do we achieve a blessed life? Mary's life provides a clear example. We must believe. We must believe that God makes the impossible things possible. Not only that, we must surrender to the work God desires to do in us and through us. Mary's life demonstrated this point as well. When the angel Gabriel told Mary she would bear the long awaited King, her simple response communicated much. Mary said, "May it be to me as you have said" (Luke 1:38).

Each day, you need to have the same attitude that was present in Mary's life so many years ago. "Lord, may it be to me as you have said." As you embrace this attitude, like Mary, you will live a blessed life in the very presence of God. The blessed life will not exclude the hard times, but it will position you to long for your real home in heaven as well as to understand that nothing is impossible for those who believe.

Think About It

Please explain the difference between a blessed life from God's perspective and a blessed life from the world's perspective. _____

_____

_____

_____

_____

Please explain how Mary's life was blessed from God's perspective. _____

_____

_____

_____

_____

Please list the crucial step you must take in order to experience the blessed life.

_____

_____

_____

_____

Are you willing to daily take this step?   YES   NO

How will this step impact your life? _____

_____

_____

_____

_____

Respond To It

Journal a prayer asking the Lord to help you view your life from His perspective of blessing as well as surrender to His plans for your life._____

_____

_____

_____

_____

_____

_____

Day 38:
A Radiant Face

"Those who look to him are radiant;
their faces are never covered with shame."

Psalm 34:5

Read It

Today I want to encourage you to take note of the temporary as well as eternal reward for living a free life in Jesus Christ. In Psalm 34:5, David described the reward in the following way: "Those who look to him are radiant; their faces are never covered with shame."

Throughout God's Word, a radiant face demonstrated something unique. It marked the fact that a person had been with God. In the Old Testament when Moses came down from Mt. Sinai after receiving the Ten Commandments, his face shone like the sun. The apostle Paul spoke of Moses' experience in the New Testament book of 2 Corinthians. As he referred to that experience, he asked the question that if the Old Covenant led Moses to have a radiant face, how much more will the New Covenant lead New Testament believers to have a radiant face? Paul's answer can be summarized in three words—so much more! (2 Corinthians 3:7–18)

As believers in Jesus Christ, we need to know that we can have radiant faces. Perhaps you have been around someone whose face glows no matter how difficult life seems. Everything about this person points to the fact that she is free—free not by the world's definition of freedom, but free by God's definition. If we want to know what makes this person free, the answer lies in the Old Testament story of Moses. She speaks with God.

As believers, we have the living, breathing Holy Spirit living inside of us and have the opportunity to be in constant communication with our Father. We do not have to go to the top of a mountain to speak to God. Nor do we have to go through someone else like the Israelites did in order to hear from God. Under the New Covenant, we have direct access to God through Christ! We can be in constant communication with our heavenly Father. As we take advantage of the opportunity to continually meet with God, we will live in freedom and our faces will be radiant. It can't help but happen.

If you are wondering if the absence of conversation with God can lead to the opposite of today's truth, let me assure you it can. Forsaking communication with God heightens the possibility of sin making its way into our lives and makes us susceptible to worry, confusion, and shame. Then our faces will not glow with the assurances of Christ.

Dear friend, you are free to thrive as you look to Jesus every single day. Looking to God provides the path to freedom and readies you for the day when you will see Jesus face to face. As you long for your heavenly home, take advantage of the opportunity to talk to God. Know that your time with Him will affect the way you live, the way you act, the way you feel, and even the way you look. Live a radiant life on this earth and know that one day you will see Jesus face to face. When that happens, your face will finally be transformed into His likeness, and there will no longer be a struggle to focus on Jesus or your real home.

Think About It

Do you know someone whose face is radiant regardless of the circumstances of life? If so, please describe this person. _____

_____

_____

_____

_____

Have you ever considered the truth that talking to God will transform your life and give you a radiant face? Please explain your answer._____

_____

_____

_____

_____

Please describe the crucial element of having a radiant face. _____

_____

_____

_____

Today, how do you plan to stay in constant communication with the Father?_____

_____

_____

_____

Respond To It

Journal a prayer asking the Lord to grant you a radiant face._____

_____

_____

_____

_____

_____

_____

Day 39:
A Finished Race

"However, I consider my life worth nothing to me, if only I may finish the race and complete the task the Lord Jesus has given me—the task of testifying to the gospel of God's grace."

Acts 20:24

Read It

These words, spoken by the apostle Paul, were simple but not easy. I think if Paul had written this verse in the form of a "to do" list, it might have read:

- "Forsake my life."
- "Be sure to run a good race."
- "Run with consistency—finish as strong as I began."
- "Along the way, share God's grace with everyone I meet."

What a great "to do" list! Each point is emphasized in Acts 20:24. These points must have changed the focus of Paul's life. In the end, these points enabled Paul to live his life with a longing for his real home. As he forsook the things of this world, he lived for the moment when he would see Jesus face to face.

As we long for that day in our lives, our daily "to do" list should reflect a clear focus. We too should be able to say, "Each day I will forsake my life." This will lead us to turn from the things of the world that often bind us up and enable us to instead live for the things of Christ. We will be forced to give up the world's definition of freedom—doing what I want to do, when I want to do it, and having the resources available to make it happen. We will be challenged to embrace God's definition of freedom, which involves Christ in every area of our lives.

Our daily "to do" list should also say, "Each day, be sure to run a good race." We each run a good race when we view our relationship with God as a marathon, not a sprint. A sprint calls for a sudden burst of energy that leaves as fast as it came. In contrast, a marathon calls for a steady flow of consistent energy that enables us to go the distance.

Think about a time when you fell into the trap of living like you were running a sprint instead of a marathon. Perhaps life was especially busy, or you took on a tremendous amount of responsibility, leaving you with little hope of doing anything well. Continually living your life like a sprint leads to burnout because there is just not enough energy supply to meet the energy demand. We right this wrong by living with the same focus it takes to run a marathon. This focus brings balance and discipline as we weigh what should and should not be in our lives. In the end, the discipline of living with a "marathon mindset" enables us to finish as strong as we began.

Not long ago, I sat in my home church and watched a DVD presentation about a senior adult mission trip. The trip required a long bus ride, hands-on work, and a thriving love for Jesus Christ. As I watched my brothers and sisters in Christ who were in their seventies and eighties, I was moved to tears. I was challenged by the fact that my brothers and sisters in Christ were serving the Lord long after many of their friends had quit, and I said to myself, "I want to be just like that." Without a doubt, marathon living allows us to live a long, consistent life for Jesus Christ.

Finally, our "to do" list should say, "Along the way, share God's grace with everyone I meet!" I believe the greatest evidence of a longing for our eternal home is seen in the desire to tell others about that home. Imagine having the grandest destination and keeping it a secret. This situation happens each time we forget or forsake sharing Christ. Believers in Jesus Christ have the absolute best destination in front of them—heaven! This truth should be so much on our minds every day that we can't help but share Christ with those we meet.

Think About It

Of the four "to do's" on Paul's list, which one challenges you and why? _____

_____

_____

What do you need to do on a very practical level to accomplish the four "to do's" discussed in today's devotion?

1. _____

_____

2. _____

_____

3. _____

_____

4. _____

_____

Respond To It

Journal a prayer asking the Lord to hold you accountable to the tasks you just described.

_____

_____

_____

_____

Day 40:
A Final Home

"Then I saw a new heaven and a new earth, for the first heaven and the first earth had passed away, and there was no longer any sea. I saw the Holy City, the new Jerusalem, coming down out of heaven from God, prepared as a bride beautifully dressed for her husband. And I heard a loud voice from the throne saying, "Now the dwelling of God is with men, and he will live with them. They will be his people, and God himself will be with them and be their God. He will wipe every tear from their eyes. There will be no more death or mourning or crying or pain, for the old order of things has passed away."

Revelation 21:1–4

Read It

Today I want to encourage you to allow the words of Revelation 21:1–4 to focus your attention on your final home. Dear friend, a day is coming when the things of this world—the things that we currently see, hear, touch, smell, and enjoy—will pass away. On that day we will see, hear, touch, smell, and enjoy things we cannot begin to imagine! Knowing this truth should draw our eyes heavenward as we long for the day when there will be no more death, mourning, crying, or pain, a day when the old order of things has passed away and a new order has finally arrived.

Living with our eyes focused on heaven changes the way we live on this earth. We can have:

- A clear focus. This world is not our home—we are just passing through.
- A reachable goal. One day we will see Jesus face to face—it will happen.
- A final destination. Heaven will be the place where we spend all of eternity. We will never leave that wonderful home.

A powerful promise. Once we arrive in heaven, there will be no sin, hurt, shame, guilt, doubt, confusion, sickness, pain, or death. We will live at peace with God and at peace with men. We will never have to worry about a single thing.

Heaven—there is no place like it, and there is no substitute for it. Our daily focus should be on heaven. When this occurs, the things of this world fade, and the promises of Christ are magnified. Spiritual fruit like peace, assurance, and great hope take the place of worry, doubt and concern as we view our lives as temporary on this earth and eternal in glory.

Galatians 5:1 states: "It is for freedom that Christ has set us free. Stand firm, then, and do not let yourselves be burdened again by a yoke of slavery." This verse sums up every concept that has been presented in *Free to Thrive*. Christ sets the believer free! Living in the freedom Christ provides brings peace into our lives. The effect of this peace is confidence in God and a desire to focus on our final home in heaven. No longer does the world tell us what freedom means. Freedom is found in living our lives in total abandon to Jesus Christ. Living in total abandon to Jesus requires that we surrender every aspect of our being to God. This surrender brings forth a trust in the Lord as His plans permeate every aspect of our lives, yielding a confident spirit that willingly fights for freedom and longs for the day when we will see Jesus face to face.

Freedom. This world will never understand it and never fully provide it. In Christ, real freedom can be found. God's desire for you is to walk in the freedom He provides! Dear sister, through Christ, you are free to thrive!

Think About It

Do you look forward to your final home in heaven? If so, please explain. _____

_____

_____

_____

Of the four truths presented in today's devotion, circle the ones that bring a sense of peace to your heart, then explain the reasons in the space below.

1. We have a clear focus. This world is not our home—we are just passing through.

2. We have a reachable goal. One day we will see Jesus face to face—it will happen.

3. We have a final destination. Heaven will be the place where we spend all of eternity. We will never leave that wonderful home.

4. We have a powerful promise. Once we arrive in heaven, there will be no sin, hurt, shame, guilt, doubt, confusion, sickness, pain, or death. We will live at peace with God and at peace with men. We will never have to worry.

_____

_____

_____

Respond To It

Journal a prayer asking the Lord to help you live for your final home._____

_____

_____

_____

_____

_____

Endnotes

Week 1 Day 1

- Yoke: Merriam-Webster's On-line Dictionary, "yoke," May 10, 2011.

Week 2 Day 7

- Demolish: Bible Navigator Bible Software (Nashville, TN: Holman Interactive), *Strong's Greek and Hebrew Dictionary,* # 2507, January 15, 2011.
- Arguments: Spiros Zodhiates, *The Key Word Study Bible*, (Chattanooga, TN: AMG Publishers, 1996) # 3361, 1646.
- Pretension: Bible Navigator Bible Software, *Vine's Expository Dictionary of Old and New Testament Words.* # G5313, May 10, 2011.
- Take captive: Ibid., #G163.

Week 2 Day 9

- Honor: Spiros Zodhiates, *The Key Word Study Bible*, (Chattanooga, TN: AMG Publishers, 1996) # 1518, 1611.

Week 3 Day 15

- Gaze: Merriam-Webster On-line Dictionary, "gaze," May 10, 2011.
- Glance: Merriam-Webster On-line Dictionary, "glance," May 10, 2011.

Week 8 Day 36

- Pilgrimage: Zodhiates, *The Key Word Study Bible*. (Chattanooga, TN: AMG Publishers, 1996) # 4472, 1961.

Week 8 Day 37

- Blessed: Zodhiates, *The Key Word Study Bible*. (Chattanooga, TN: AMG Publishers, 1996) # 3421, 1647.